BOX KITE

BOX KITE

PROSE POEMS
BY BAZIJU

ROO BORSON
& KIM MALTMAN

ANANSI

Published in Canada in 2016 and in
the USA in 2016 by House of Anansi Press Inc.
www.houseofanansi.com

House of Anansi Press is committed to protecting our natural environment.
As part of our efforts, the interior of this book is printed on paper made from
second-growth forests and is acid-free.

20 19 18 17 16   1 2 3 4 5

Library and Archives Canada Cataloguing in Publication

Baziju, author
Box kite : prose poems / by Baziju (Roo Borson & Kim Maltman).

Issued in print and electronic formats.
ISBN 978-1-77089-964-3 (bound).—ISBN 978-1-77089-962-9 (paperback).—
ISBN 978-1-77089-963-6 (pdf)

I. Title.

PS8603.A962B69 2016   C811'.6   C2015-907817-2
                                             C2015-907818-0

Library of Congress Control Number: 2015957631

Cover image: Baziju
Cover design: Alysia Shewchuk
Text design and typesetting: Marijke Friesen

 Canada Council   Conseil des Arts   ONTARIO ARTS COUNCIL
for the Arts   du Canada   CONSEIL DES ARTS DE L'ONTARIO

 TORONTO
ARTS
COUNCIL

*We acknowledge for their financial support of our publishing program the
Canada Council for the Arts, the Ontario Arts Council, and the Government
of Canada through the Canada Book Fund.*

Printed and bound in Canada

Having seen a kite, they all sent servants off to get their own kites. When the kites were up and had reached the end of their strings, they cut the strings, setting them loose. The loosed kites then disappeared, taking the bad luck of their owners with them.

— Loose adaptation of an incident occurring during the Poetry Club meeting in Chapter 70 of *Honglou Meng* (*The Story of the Stone* in David Hawkes's translation)

Eternal verities are always present and easily acquired; in greater jeopardy are those fragile details that make up the palpable past.

— Stephen Owen

Box Kite

I ask for the Chinese name of that flower and you tell me, then tell me about the sweet that is made for moon-viewing, wisteria blooms soaked in sugar then rolled in dough, so that I forget all about the name and will have to go to the dictionary to look it up. This is in Spadina Village, a cascade of early purple blooms down the whitewashed building across the street, some kind of a bar or bistro. This is how it goes: inside you there are pictures and in me there are others. Here is the shrub that is translated as *plum*, though we would never call it a plum except in translation. You ask if there's a word for unspoken understanding, but as usual in English there's no single word, even *silent transmission* is two, though it's often pictured as moonlight, that sudden. In any case, much of the time it is a subtle *mis*understanding that permeates everything: without misunderstanding there would be no literature, no jokes or puns. This is the flower called bleeding heart, its name reflects its structure, but at the same time refers to the death of Christ. And here is a miniature Korean flag, fallen in the street after the festivities for the World Cup, here the eight basic trigrams that combine to form all possible circumstances. You plant it upright in someone's lawn and it stirs to life. Most of us have such great feeling, but the work we do is small. Not much need for talking, but anyway there is talk.

You don't have to travel far to hear about faraway things. It was in a small restaurant called the East Garden, just a few blocks from here, for instance, that we first learned of the snow cabbages of Harbin. We'd ordered a steamer of dumplings to start, and a dish of pork and spinach in sour sauce to follow, and, by trying to practice our Mandarin, had ended up chatting with the waitress who, it turned out, was originally from Harbin. Generally, with dumplings, the cook will place a little something — slices of carrot, a slip of parchment paper, the leaves of some green vegetable — on the slats of the bamboo steamer to keep the dumplings from sticking. And so tonight, having dipped each dumpling ceremoniously in vinegar and popped the last of them into our mouths, we found ourselves left with a few old cabbage leaves, still green, but heavily wilted from the steaming. Setting down our second dish, and seeing the leaves still there, our waitress suddenly exclaimed: "We eat these where I come from — dipped in sauce . . ." and gestured to the plate of pork and spinach. Dipping our leaves into the dark brown sour sauce, under her watchful eye, we agreed they were delicious. Then, holding the empty steamer, she told us something of her childhood in Harbin.

In winter, she explained, it was impossible to buy fresh vegetables, so each fall each family would gather up a store — potatoes and turnips, but mostly cabbages. These they kept fresh by burying them in the snow once winter came. The outer leaves would freeze, but under the snow the cabbage hearts remained cool and crisp all winter long. As a child, she remembered, she'd always tired of this diet. It was only since moving far away, to a place with plenty of electricity, and a refrigerator in every house, that she'd grown nostalgic for that steamed winter cabbage, whose leaves somehow acquired a special flavour in the freezing process. Even back home, she said, where everyone had fridges now, it had become almost impossible to find that dish, and many of her friends also remembered it with fondness.

As she spoke, I could imagine the family gathered around on a freezing winter day, dipping cabbage leaves in some delicious sauce, making (as we say) a virtue of necessity. One could, she said, go out of one's way to make them now, but somehow ... And I understood what she meant, for it would hardly be the same. Were I to move to a distant country, learn the language and attempt to cope, I too, no doubt, surprised by strangers able to speak a few words of my native tongue, would suddenly come alive with stories of the old ways.

And which of the marvellous foods of my childhood, I wonder, would I choose to describe, pausing a moment to chat to those interesting strangers?

It began with a shortcut up the mountain, recommended by a local shopkeeper whose premises we'd entered, looking for directions, when the last stop on the bus route turned out to be, not within sight of the temple as we'd been expecting, but instead off on a minor side street, just before the edge of town. It was midday, and the shop empty of customers, and having heard our halting Chinese, he'd kindly taken time to draw a sketch-map with his finger on the counter, chatting to us all the while.

Oddly enough, the "shortcut" turned out to involve following the newer, paved roads rather than some well-worn local footpath. We were well on our way then, passing the small cascades of trash and wastewater which spilled out down the slopes when, around a bend, a great sea eagle, even then still in the midst of taking off, rose up before us. It had apparently been sunning itself on the road and was no doubt as startled as we were by this chance encounter. Now, dipping one wing, it floated off effortlessly down the mountain. Soon we spotted what appeared to be the first of the hiking trails, snaking off to the left past a few ramshackle buildings among the pines. It was at this moment that a man, of our age or a little older, yet apparently quite unaffected by the summer heat, came striding up behind us.

Stripped to the waist, he cut a figure like that of Li Bai in the poem "Summer Day in the Mountains"

("Waving my white feather fan," etc.), though rather than waving a white feather fan he wore ordinary trousers and hiking boots, and greeted us with an expansive wave of the arm, and smile. A moment later a woman appeared, petite and comparatively demure in a pantsuit and medium-high-heeled dress shoes, and took her place beside him. The four of us compared notes in a languageless, hand-waving sort of way, and when it became apparent that our routes lay in separate directions (for ours still followed the road), we wished them well and set off on our own — though rather slowly at first for, having turned to monitor their progress, we found ourselves instead now watching in astonishment as, with his wife's assistance, and out of the following unlikely materials, to wit:

> two faded brown hand towels
> two lengths of string
> four wooden clothes pegs

our fellow mountaineer assembled for himself an impromptu hiking shirt. One hand towel was hung in front, the other in the back, and with the lengths of string for shoulder straps, held in place at the junctures by the wooden clothes pegs, the shirt was at last complete. Our vision of Li Bai then took off at a great rate up the mountain, followed closely by his wife, the pair of them rapidly vanishing among the pines.

We continued along the road, which blended into another, smaller road winding its way upward, until we reached the base of a stone stairway, where we rested. Climbing again past several successive landings, stopping for breath at each, we arrived at last at the relatively level grounds of the temple. From here we could look out over surprisingly green and hilly country, the eagle's vistas of lowland, hill, and valley spreading all the way to the blue in the distance, which was the sea. Straight down the steep slope we could just make out the city of Taibei, with its many factories, which appeared through the lens of high clear air to be spun entirely of golden haze.

The main door of the temple was by now thrown open for the day, and through it we could see, beyond the darkened entranceway, the ornate trappings of the grand halls of the inner temple, in the midst of which the preparations for some Daoist ceremony were evidently well in progress. Disinclined to enter, we continued, following the echo of a woman's footsteps on the stone tiles clockwise to the back side of the temple building. Here the terrace extended to a low, carved stone wall, which looked out over a gentler side of the mountain, itself sculpted into terraces, on which people of diverse ages could be seen engaged, each separately, in exercises which appeared neither martial nor devotional, some performing dancelike movements in a trance of attention, others, seated here and there, bolt upright, eyes shut, still others — all of them young men, I noticed — walking barefoot back and forth with studied steps over a bed of inlaid stones. The stones were not sharp, but rounded like beach stones, and nearby, on a metal sign, a diagram in the shape of a footprint, decorated with swirling lines and characters whose meaning we were at a loss to understand, had been provided for the visitor, by way of explanation.

Beyond the temple grounds proper, a narrow boardwalk led into a forest of bamboo. The walkway zigzagged this way and that, while high above us stripes of light, cast through the canopy, played here and there across the trunks, which teetered, in their great height, like the strings of some enormous harp forever on the verge of trembling into sound. For some time we found ourselves walking alternately in front of, then behind, an old man and his grandson, who continued chatting softly to each other, even as they fell into single file to overtake or let us pass, apart from this not once acknowledging our presence. At one point we passed what appeared to be a forester's or nurseryman's home: in the loosely fenced enclosure two men were squatting in a ragged garden potting some leafy plants, while water from a pipe flooded the ground nearby. By now the boardwalk had given way to a dirt path, which ran crookedly through mixed deciduous and pine forest.

The guidebook we'd brought along had already proved itself considerably out of date, and in place of maps had a penchant for verbal directions, which were not only puzzling, but often at odds with whatever signs, roads, or buildings we actually found ourselves in front of. At that moment what stood before us was a steep path leading down into a deep ravine — beyond which we could make out, through the trees, the outline of a second temple, perched high on the other side. Partly shrouded in bamboo scaffolding, it appeared to be undergoing major reconstruction. A lot of lumber was lying about, and some large rolls of wire. We'd already been debating whether to go on, given the time and absence of a proper map, when from off to one side who should appear but our hiker and his wife, laughing with pleasure to see us. The man's hiking shirt was soaked through, and even his wife's elegant forehead was lightly pearled with dew. Gesturing with a sweep of the arm, he indicated that the second temple could be reached along the side path they'd emerged from, adding, via supplementary gestures, that this route was to be preferred over the more direct but steeper one which led through the ravine. And with that they were off again, at speed, heading back the way we'd come.

The path continued for some distance, growing ever more entangled, until finally, still not within sight of the temple, we decided to turn back — though not without a feeling that, in doing so, in having in this way betrayed some minor trust, a line certain to lead to future disappointment had been crossed.

Arriving at the terraces again, we found the crowd much larger and more lively than before. Couples, families with young children, elderly men and women on their own, all were milling about enjoying the views, snapping photos, or else taking their ease, sipping from cups of tea which, now that it was mid-afternoon, were being sold from a small handcart. Passing the bed of stones, then circling back, removing our shoes and socks beneath that enigmatic diagram, I realized I'd seen those swirling lines before, on the elongated sole of a statue of the reclining Buddha. As for the mountaineer and his wife, we never saw them again.

Li Bai, of the Tang Dynasty, as far as is known, could not have set foot on the island of Taiwan, though at any banquet in the city, if you ask your fellow guests for a poem, what they are likely to recite is one of his. *Summer day in the mountains. Idly waving a white feather fan, stripped to the waist in the green woods, I take off my headcloth, hang it from a rocky cliff, let the wind from the pines sprinkle my head.*

Coming on this poem again, I find myself remembering once more that temple in the mountains.

Bi shan si, as it is called — Green Mountain Temple, the Temple of the Emerald Hills. We've left the bustle of the city for the day and overhead the clouds are racing. Like the travellers from some ancient tale, we've set out again, oblivious, as at the start of all such seemingly quite ordinary journeys, in which fortune, which we may not even recognize as fortune, smiles — the open view behind us, and the pine wind blowing gently at each turning of the road.

Jilong was every shade of grey in the rain. Red-grey, yellow-grey, green-grey, grey. It had been raining all the way from Hualian, where there were mudslides. In Hualian we'd spent the night in a hotel decorated with red velvet and imitation stained glass, overlooking an intersection which shrieked the whole night through with gunning motorbikes and small trucks blaring out presidential campaign ads, live, through loudspeakers, hand-held or mounted on their roofs. And now the rain-soaked sea, the blocky cement structures of the sugar towns, a cement-coloured crescent of wet beach, this or that hillside grotto of cycads, ferns the size of small houses — each time the train was swallowed up in a tunnel the world went black, swaying and rocking, only to be resurrected again the next moment. Now, at last, all this was behind us and, now heavy, now light, now drenching, now middling, the rain continued....

A map we'd picked up at the station had shown several hotels, and we'd made our way now to the nearest of these. A sailor took a swig from a mickey-sized paper bag as I squeezed past in the narrow corridor which served as a lobby, and into the tiny elevator. Passing by an open door along the way, I caught sight of one of the other guests, a young woman talking on a cellphone. Our room-to-be had an actual porthole for a window and beautiful, mildewed wainscoting, which gave off an odd air of dampness and chill. And so for the second time I passed by the young woman, who sat perched in her miniskirt on a matching circular bed, still talking softly on her cellphone, and rode back down to the lobby to return the room key and decline the room, and then we slogged our way again through the rain, dragging our luggage up and down over the labyrinthine series of pedestrian overpasses.

After tea, a hot shower, and some desultory television in a second (this time, mercifully acceptable) hotel called the Kodak, whose sewing kit I still carry with me, we made our way downstairs to the hotel restaurant. What we wanted was a bowl of rice, a green vegetable, possibly some bean curd, above all to avoid having to venture out again into that pouring rain. The menu, when it finally arrived, however, spoke more of the hotel's elevated image of itself than of the contents of its dishes, being one of those composed almost entirely of gracious yet curious literary allusions, most of them unknown to us, and only a handful bearing names into which words we recognized for food had been allowed to slip. Among these was a dish called *Xishi Doufu*.

This (leaving aside the doufu for the moment), although also an allusion, was at least one that we recognized. Xishi: legendary beauty of the Warring States period. Favourite concubine to the last, doomed king of the state of Wu, so bewitching that, languishing in her company, he allowed his whole kingdom to be overrun and lost. Rice, a vegetable, and *Xishi Doufu* it would have to be then, although why Xishi, and what this doufu that now bore her name might turn out to consist of, we would have to wait and see.

Often when I think of doufu, I remember the novel *A Small Town Called Hibiscus* by the Chinese writer Gu Hua. The novel is set in a poor village in Hunan during the sixties and seventies, a period of great upheaval throughout the country. It makes frequent and lavish references to an incredibly tender bean curd, a bean curd which in fact turns out to be not exactly bean curd, but a "bean curd" contrived out of the sweepings of rice powder gathered from the storeroom floor. The bean curd vendor, Yuyin, has been declared a "rich peasant," dispossessed, and forced to make her living selling bean curd on the streets. Throughout the novel, numerous servings of this "doufu" are dolloped out, steaming hot, into bowls, and doused with chili oil and green onion. Each appearance in the novel made me famished — so much so that, ever since, every unknown bean curd dish appearing on a Chinese menu makes me once more long for it.

At the end of Gu Hua's novel it is 1979, and Yuyin has, at last, been rehabilitated. Her tormentor, Wang Qiushe, has gone mad and wanders the streets, calling out endlessly for yet another revolutionary political movement, long after the era of such movements, and the devastation they (and he) have brought to other people's lives, has passed. I thought again of Yuyin's doufu as we waited (patiently, and for some time — like the King of the doomed state of Wu, we joked) for our order to arrive.

And now before us stood a dish of *Xishi Doufu*. The cubes so white they seemed almost translucent, so delicate they registered even the slight shocks of the waiters passing, unobtrusively as always, near our table. The tremulous cubes slid away at the touch of the serving spoon and, upon being lifted with chopsticks, would pause a moment and then break in half.

Often since then I have thought of that dish, though in my mind it is now hopelessly entangled with the doufu of Gu Hua's story. Thus, on occasion, when I come upon doufu listed in a restaurant menu, I find myself not only remembering the town of Hibiscus and the doufu of those revolutionary times, but wondering whether I might not, like the legendary last King of the once-great, now long-vanished state of Wu, be living through the last days of some great tragedy I am as yet completely unaware of. Perhaps this is why the story of ordering *Xishi Doufu* in the restaurant of the Kodak Hotel, in the port city of Jilong, on the northeast corner of the island of Taiwan, has stayed with me, and why I am now writing it down — to (as Gu Hua says in his postscript, reflecting on the times he lived through) "comfort, encourage, mock and explain myself."

Long ago, before there was even a single road, there was a village of nine families, accessible only by boat. Once a month or so, depending on the weather, a boat would bring supplies to the village. These would be bundled up into nine portions, one for each of the families living there. Then one day gold was discovered, a road was built, and the town grew continuously until the gold ran out. Afterwards the road remained, but one by one the buildings were abandoned, and the town became a village once more, populated largely by ghosts. Meanwhile, prosperity arrived elsewhere on the island, and the old-style buildings, so beautiful to look at but uncomfortable, it was said, to live in, were replaced by all the trappings of a modern urban world. Now people come back to the village to see such sights again. Travelling there, you may find yourself thinking of those POWs who worked the mines nearby in World War II, or of those nine families before that, largely cut off from the world. If you go, there is a beautiful old teahouse, in the Qing style, and outside, the makers of local delicacies once more lay out their trays of taro and sweet potato balls. Most travellers come in tour groups, but it is also possible to come by local bus. From Jilong station, take the route that heads toward Ruifang. Ruifang — the scent of daphne. Halfway there, you'll have arrived. If you stay on into evening, the rain may let up, and you may hear the sound of the sea again, once more see supplies being unloaded, and those ghosts, whose homes these were, walking the streets. The name of the town is Jiufen, or Nine Pieces, and it lies high in the hills, in the mountainous region to the northeast of Taibei.

I'd been trying to look up a reference to the *ba gua* for my friend Yam Lau, who is interested in such things, but without any luck, for though I'd seen it mentioned somewhere in the writings of Lu Yu, and though the partial translation of a diary of his journey down the Yangtze was all I'd read of his work, each time I picked up the book to look again I remained as puzzled as before, and the *ba gua* were nowhere to be found. At the time another friend and I happened to be in the midst of planning our own trip down that same river, to see the famous sights along the banks of the Three Gorges before they too disappeared. One more year and many such sights, including the *ba gua*, would be swallowed up in the damming of the river. But before we could settle on an itinerary, the Yangtze swelled, turning the flood year into one of the most disastrous in decades.

The Yangtze in flood is like a snake swallowing a rat: the bulge moves steadily and swiftly and a very long way before dispersing. The river is so long and its progress so steady that remarkably accurate predictions can be made as to the time of day the floodwaters will reach such-and-such a city three or four days hence. If it's true that what we know of a place veils our eyes before we see it, this must be especially true of those places renowned in literature — and so it may be that, having read Lu Yu's diary,

I've already seen all I will ever know of that region of the Yangtze. In any case, the news clips of the flooding were enough to dissuade us, and so it was that after some time we found ourselves not on one of the great ships that travel the river, but instead crammed into a tiny tourist boat in the middle of West Lake, veering toward the small islets which in August are willow-green and edged with flowers.

It is a pleasant thing to find oneself in the middle of West Lake in the middle of one's life, to consider the view, and to imagine what is left of one's days stretching out before one toward some imagined horizon, along with the various islets and purpose-built causeways. It must be the effect of this most spacious of lakes in their midst that makes the inhabitants of Hangzhou so serious and easygoing. As one resident, abashed on behalf of his city, and with a beautiful lazy smile, described it, the pace of Hangzhou is "a little slow." In the heat of summer the lakeside paths are crowded with bicyclists and local youth, and with tour groups being shown the sights. The paths are everywhere bordered by flowering gardens, and the gardens are aglitter with butterflies: every flower with its butterfly, and every butterfly a flower, as they say, that has taken to the air. The gardens are adorned with ponds, and the ponds, in turn, with bridges, beneath which the carp gather, opening their mouths in enormous zeroes before the gaping tourists, then winding their way back and forth, braiding the invisible currents with orange blurs and streaks.

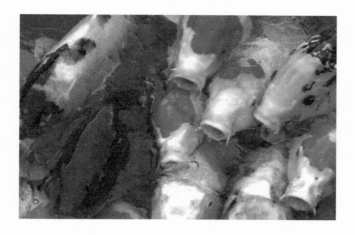

Earlier in the day, walking the length of the Bai Causeway, we'd stopped for a moment to take a look at the plaque which commemorates the poet Bai Juyi — or was it the Su Causeway, named in honour of Su Dongpo, poet of the Song and governor of Hangzhou, under whose orders this second causeway was built? At any rate, we were hot and thirsty, and a faint breeze, stirred up as if by the pleasure boats that passed nearby, seemed to jostle the words from our mouths as we read.

Since coming to Hangzhou, I'd been looking in bookstores for an English version of the works of Su Dongpo, in particular the piece "In Praise of Pork," and so had often thought of Su, a man still revered for his good governance, even a thousand years after his death (something that seems incredible in our age), not to mention his stature as a poet and essayist. Asked about Su that night, and *Dongpo rou*, the dish named after him, our waiter, in a state of some excitement, hurried off, returning with the manager, who told us, in quite gorgeous English, that it was to Su Dongpo we owed the beauty of the scene before us — cajoling a reluctant populace to take part in the dredging of the lake, their regard for him in this case supplemented by the promise of a dish of *Dongpo rou* to end each working day. Needless to say, this story proved an excellent enticement, and we ordered *Dongpo rou* — although the truth, we've since heard, is less fanciful: that local farmers, grateful for the beautification of their lake, made him gifts of pork, which Su, reciprocating, ordered cooked in "Dongpo style," inviting everyone to feast.

Hence (in any case) *Dongpo rou*, a dish which by its nature might account for Su Dongpo's substantial girth, recorded in the portraits of the time. A small clay pot, in which a single square of rich pork (the meat interleaved with layers of fat) bubbles in a sauce of dark sweet soy and yellow Shaoxing wine, is placed before each diner. Even the layers of fat, with the infusion of this sauce, become addictive, so much so that we could well imagine joining the helpless populace reporting to the lake each morning.

Like the carp that follow one another through the water, tourists, as a rule, follow Hangzhou with Suzhou, or vice versa. Even the old proverbs refer to the two, Su-Hang, in a single breath. And so we too moved on, spending several nights in one of Suzhou's tourist inns. Outside our window green tangerines, another local specialty, were ripening. Suzhou is famous for its canals and gardens: the Garden of the Master of Nets, the Blue Wave Pavilion, the Garden of the Humble Administrator — the latter built in the early sixteenth century by a corrupt Ming official, for his retirement. And indeed we spent our time there most pleasantly despite the heat, languorously wandering the various gardens, not thinking once of the soon-to-be-flooded Gorges, and the trip we'd failed to take.

Some months after returning from Suzhou, Hangzhou, and the various other places we visited, not one of them along the Yangtze, I found myself still troubled, having discovered nothing more about the *ba gua* for my friend Yam Lau — beyond, that is, what anyone could find searching the internet. That a third-century strategist named Zhuge Liang designed a battle array based on the eight trigrams, the *ba gua*. That this mazelike design has been seen to reappear, century after century, at a particular point along the shoals of the Yangtze whenever the water level is low. That such a marvel could be made to simply vanish from the world. . . .

Still painted on my mind is a picture of the trip we might have taken down that river. Sitting on deck in the river-breeze, we're leisurely peeling the famous oranges that are grown along the banks and tossing the peels to the fish, invisible in those most muddy and jadelike of waters. I suppose there is one Yangtze in Lu Yu, and that there would be another were we able to look at the river directly, and that these two must perpetually interfere — but it is as though, in my being unable to find it, the reference to the *ba gua* has already disappeared in the floodwaters, either the floods of that year or of the subsequent year, in which the man-made flood rises and buries all such sights. And then one day, idly dangling my arm over the side of the bed, picking up the book by its cover, I came upon the *ba gua* entry — on the last page, as it turns out, of the diary of that journey.

I think of my friend Yam Lau in the quiet before snow, adjusting his camera to take a photo of the moon out his window. The moon out his window can now be seen from any computer screen in the world. In some roundabout way I have him to thank for our trip to Hangzhou. In such a way, at any rate, these thoughts of mine come and go, following one upon another as though intent on some undiscoverable pattern. At times it's as though I've left myself behind on one of those small garden bridges, or in one of the boats that speed across the mirror surface of West Lake, watching the future all but disappear. But then, to give myself heart, I'll step out for a moment to have a look at what I think of now as Yam Lau's moon: worn down to a smooth brilliance, with a tracery of shadow — and the maze, it seems, is made.

It was a small sandalwood fan. Too small to be of any use against the summer heat, too crudely made to stand up to much use, it lay, still folded, in a summer-dampened cardboard box beneath the glass countertop in the gift shop of the Garden of the Master of Nets.

The day was hot, and the walls, hung with watercolours and calligraphic scrolls, wavered with the breezes that wandered in from time to time through the open doors, unmooring many thousands of brushstrokes. I'd been meaning to find some small gift for a friend back home, and the fan, lifted out from its box and spread open, radiated a spicy fragrance, memento of a place he'd likely never see.

The old part of the city of Suzhou remains, as in the past, a tranquil backwater of canals and laneways. Many small family homes still line the streets, though the famous walled "gardens" — elaborate residences dating back, in some cases, to the eleventh or twelfth centuries, and built by government officials in anticipation of a comfortable retirement — have long since been taken over by the state and opened to the public. In such a way the state, albeit in an earlier incarnation and by indirect means, could be said to have constructed the gardens for its own future use.

My friend had always had a fondness for these gardens, whose images he'd seen in books, and delighted especially in their names, exclaiming time and again over his favourites. Not only the Garden of the Master of Nets but the Garden for Lingering In, the Carefree Garden, the Garden of the Humble Administrator — though in this last case the vast mansion and extensive grounds of the "garden" in question, constructed from the proceeds of a long, and famously corrupt, career, would seem to represent a somewhat unexpected version of the notion of humility. Walking among ranks of intricately gnarled miniature trees or extravagant displays of peonies, we could imagine the elegant pastimes to which such a one might devote his remaining years. Nearby, prize goldfish, goggle-eyed or with bulbous crenellated heads of red or black sateen, or trailing filmy appendages that twisted and floated about them like dancers' veils, barely resembling the fins and tails of generations past, could be seen swimming pair by pair in decorative tubs in the shade of a trellis, oblivious, apparently, to the forms that even flesh can be made to assume. It is in such diverse ways that the gardens of Suzhou make visible the longing for an image of tranquility which (by construction) lies always in the viewer's past. Here or there a broom, or rake, leans gracefully against a wall, carp weave past one another in the shadows underneath a bridge. But beyond the general air of jaded hopefulness, the half-neglected beauty of the painted latticework and zigzag corridors of inlaid stone, one can sense the necessary recklessness of a former time.

✤

Much is made in the older literature of the tension between the pressures, and duty, of public service, and the desire to retire and live simply in the countryside. For the traditional scholar-bureaucrats who wrote these works, the sense of obligation — to society, as well as to one's family and descendants — was further complicated by the not-inconsiderable entitlements of public office. Whether to take up, late in life, an academic post, with its sundry duties and superfluous rigours, at a time when those his own age were already contemplating retirement, or else to retire directly, as it were, to the countryside, where the necessities of life might be had more cheaply — such analogous, if not entirely identical, anxieties now too confronted my friend, who had long ago committed himself to the ever-changing life of art.

This restlessness had grown of late into a full-fledged preoccupation. For weeks he'd been busying himself quite happily with real estate ads and building codes, sketching architectural plans in a preliminary way on coffee-house napkins as if they were ideas for paintings. Already he'd picked out an area of countryside adjacent to the wine district yet not too far outside the city, and with its own local name: the Short Hills. "A long walk in the Short Hills" is how he put it on those days when he favoured immediate retirement, envisioning a future free of our institutions of higher learning — the posturing before whose former virtues, unmade by necessity, had once more filled him with grief. Yet at the same time he relished, in his capacity as temporary lecturer, what contact he had with students, and through them the future life of art. His students, in turn, and without any outside encouragement, had begun noting down and compiling his spur-of-the-moment "sayings," oddities and decrees tossed off in the heat of a lecture and abandoned without further ado. These they would pass from hand to hand, gathering spontaneously in the halls or meeting for discussion over beer or coffee, convinced that some further understanding might be gleaned from the fragments, and the wider curriculum they implied. In this way they were able to pursue their studies with a diligence worthy of an older notion of the university, and an excitement all their own.

The Garden of the Master of Nets, whose Late Spring Studio courtyard has been replicated, stone for stone and tile for tile, in the Astor Court of the Metropolitan Museum of Art in New York City, has long been known as the smallest and most gemlike of Suzhou's extant gardens, and hence as a favourite among artists. The long metaphorical history associated with fishing nets in disciplines as far-flung as philosophy, linguistics and literature doubtless played a role in its naming, but as well, for me, there is a private association. Puzzling over the netlike structures which appeared again and again in my friend's paintings, and upon which he declined to comment further, I'd come to think of him, too, as a kind of Master of Nets: one who, at least where art was concerned, consistently eschewed the politics of compromise — to the point where, on occasion, his very livelihood was in danger. At night sometimes, woken by worries of my own, I'd sit up in bed, surmising that my friend too was awake, far across the city, silently reciting this or that saying from the old poems.

Heaven's mesh is supposed to be wide,
but my growing old still got caught in it.

So it was the hours would pass, an endless traffic of words and phrases, half-completed thoughts that, one by one, would rise up, turning and drifting about one another, held aloft as if by unseen random gusts, only to be blown away, or reappear again a moment later — and it would seem to me that we were doomed then, each of us alone beside a sleeping spouse, to ponder in this way indefinitely quite ordinary problems, which in the dark admit of no solution. Adrift in this spectral world, beset by possibilities, at last the strangest notions would come over me: that *we* are the posthumous life of art (for instance), reconstituted in these very bodies and minds — and only then would I fall asleep once more, consoled by this, or some other equally preposterous insight, which, even then I sensed, would vanish with the dawn. So it was that I grew used to thinking of my friend's dilemma in the city of lost hours the night had become, and determined, on arriving in Suzhou, to bring back a souvenir in recognition of his bond with that place. I like to think that the little fan, roughly hewn and loosely sewn, set lovingly by his wife inside a cabinet at home, might somehow be of use, spending its fragrance among cups and glasses and other miscellany.

✤

The Garden of the Master of Nets and Garden of the Humble Administrator have by now achieved iconic status, and the self-perpetuating fame that comes with it. They are listed among the *Four Famous Gardens of Suzhou*, the *Eight Famous Gardens of China*, and are certain to appear on every traveller's itinerary, in every guidebook. But my own favourite among the gardens of Suzhou is the one we saw first, the very afternoon of our arrival.

We'd come by train from Shanghai and, after some confusion, found a taxi to the gates of our hotel. It had been suffocating in the station, and the taxi ride and overpowering humidity had left us drenched with sweat. Checking in at last, we'd set our bags down in the pleasant air-conditioned room, which looked out on a scene of grass and dappled shade, and trees on which hung still-green local tangerines — and then my spouse, untiring as ever, had led us instantly back out into the August heat and through the back streets to the nearest of the ancient gardens. It was the day before his birthday, and we spent the hour or two that remained dawdling and resting in the blue-green shade of the Blue Wave Pavilion, stopping every few steps to sit, hand in hand, in this oldest of the city's gardens.

Wisteria had climbed everywhere, making one of those classical scenes of a type depicted in Chinese porcelains of the nineteenth century, meant for sale to the European market — and reminding me of the trellis by the back door of my childhood home. Before she died, my mother told me she had only two regrets, neither of which involved the gardens of Suzhou. Still, I couldn't help imagining she would have loved to have seen this place with her own eyes. There is an old poem from the Tang or Song I must track down again sometime. It describes a scene like this, and though they've not been mentioned to this point, ends in translation with the line

And the rocks, wild and forgetful —

In the Blue Wave Pavilion I found myself thinking of that line again, looking out onto the "borrowed scenery," which lies outside the garden but is visually contained by it. That this borrowed scenery is different now from that the builders once intended does not compromise the beauty of the garden. Or my artist friend's delight in the idea, if it comes to that. For some time I'd been sitting, watching as a white moth struggled up one side of my sandal strap, then down the other, and musing about human intelligence. How much of our time is spent in forms of half-frenetic daydreaming, telling stories where friends, the past, and we ourselves appear as characters. How, over the centuries, a garden such as this would many times have fallen into disrepair, only to be restored again, each time toward a different image of perfection.

It was some days later, in the grounds of the Garden of the Master of Nets, that I came across the small sandalwood fan. By then, having spent — as is sometimes said in the journals of those early European travellers bold enough to venture inland from the comfort of the foreign quarters of the Shanghai of the twenties — "no little time" in the city's gardens, the linkage of my friend to those images seen in books, whose range of photographic reproductions spans almost the entire twentieth century, had been replaced by a linkage to something both less and more ephemeral, something more akin, that is, to the gardens themselves, at least in this, the most current of their ever-changing forms.

Each of the gardens had its own design and feel, its own reflexive intelligence as it were — yet each, too, was bound by convention. Each had its water feature, its railing over which one might gaze into some carefully constructed distance, its miniature hill or mountain built from the stone, riddled with holes, dredged from the bottom of Lake Tai. These stones were much sought after by the garden makers of the Ming and Qing and, by that time, quite rare. They would have been brought overland to Suzhou on carts, or transported by barge along the system of canals and waterways which played a central role in the commerce of the region. One Taihu "peak" is said to have required a warship and some thousand labourers to move it to the capital, occasioning much damage to the water gates and bridges in its path.

It was while musing about such historical lacunae, which lie forever in the background, but are nonetheless tangled up with the unfolding of various works of art — an issue of continual interest to my friend — that I stepped into the relative coolness of the gift shop and out of the heat that had now begun to radiate from the garden's rocks. Lifting the fan, and smelling the familiar fragrance, I wondered briefly at its provenance — if such a humble object could be said to have one. What sort of person might have made it, what fraction of a day's sustenance its sale might represent for the maker's family. There was little else of interest in the shop, and the shopkeeper moved slowly, putting his own fan down briefly to wrap the one I'd bought, his glass of tea untouched beside him in a pool of condensation on the countertop. Taking the receipt, whose red seal ink, when touched, left an inverted image on my fingertip, I stepped back out into the garden proper, where it was now close to noon. The sun was high, and the heat unrelenting, and as I walked with my companion, slowly once more circumnavigating the garden, my thoughts too wandered, finding other directions I had not anticipated.

All around, small family groups sat eating quietly, or else just resting in the shade, and various tour groups, on day trips from Shanghai, had begun to arrive. Images from Suzhou's many gardens now rose up before me. . . . Children ran here and there, eating ripe lotus seeds. A woman in peasant costume, selling whole pods, came toward us on a narrow stone bridge. On the pond two workers in makeshift craft unobtrusively continued with the harvest while nearby, at the water's edge, a young man crouched down lightly on his heels, reading a newspaper the colour of the rocks beneath him, as one after another flashes of light played over every surface. It was as if an art whose ending was as yet not fully known had all the while been played out in our presence, reaching out toward a future we would never know.

I believe I understand my friend: his hesitation and his certainty, his willingness and his unwillingness. Perhaps what makes a work of art is finally that its beauty can be reified, but not its function. We too, if it suited us, might dig up soil to make a pond, and find the leftover earth suitable for a hill; form a hill, and find its slopes suitable for a dwelling; build a dwelling, and find its walls suitable for paintings.

And the paintings?

Soon enough, in late spring as it happens, I'll be finished travelling again, and once more able to visit my friend and his wife in their studio in the city. The clematis, in pots beside the front door, will by then have reached halfway to the balcony, eagerly awaited by the cats, whose calendars are starred with such events. What new works, I wonder, will have sought to crowd their way into that space already crowded with their antecedents? What new interests?

My nature has a craving for openness — for gardens and other green places in the midst of human habitation that have gone wild, or been personalized by use. Yet when I find such a place, I wander back and forth indecisively, as if displaced from my origins, unable either to stay or go.

Not far from where I live there's a little restaurant called the Bagel Paradise. It's one of those local places that's "just the basics," where people go for breakfast or, maybe later on, one turning to the other says, "Why don't we pop over to the BP and get a bite to eat?" Along that stretch of Eglinton there's been a lot of commercial renewal the last few years. Various mid- to high-end restaurants that rise and fade with something oddly akin to the life cycle of the dandelion, full of life and vigour in the spring, but by fall, already barren, the decor dispersed to the four winds and the rigours of the repossessor. Also small specialty shops — shops representing someone's life savings, someone who's probably always wanted to be "their own boss," but with such a painful sense of what might constitute a marketable range of stock, I wonder what evil banker lurks in the background of that story. *Nails 'n' Lashes* (eight weeks from opening to papered-over windows), *The Swimsuit Shoppe* (from "OPENING SOON" to non-existence before I had a chance to even step inside), *Accessorize!* (come and gone over a brief rainy summer). But, in the midst of all this change, there's always been the Bagel Paradise. It's like an anchor, or a linchpin for the two halves of the neighbourhood, a turnstile where the wealthy from the north of it can, over breakfast and investment chatter, pass and nod in recognition to the other regulars from west and south of them, or banter with the owner, Bob, and feel that something around them has continued unchanged — though of course there are many new conveniences, welcomed by all, along the strip now.

But what exactly is it that remains unchanged? The drugstore with the Warhol prints is closed, the friendly owner with the outrageous prices finally retired and headed south, no one to take over the business with such a small space, and Pharma Plus across the street — though the coffee at the new Starbucks that replaced it is a big improvement over anything before. Likewise Forman's, the old "Men's Shop," that seemed like such a fixture and always reminded me of small prairie towns, Moose Jaw or Medicine Hat, for example — being the sort of good, stable business "there'll always be a call for," a fact of life, like the Cold War, or the Berlin Wall. Or Chadwick's Fine Foods — and actually, in truth, they were pretty fine, though of the sort to be purchased and picked at in small parcels — and they understood the market and location long before the others, only they had the bad luck to be ahead of both their time and the drop in interest rates, and had to pack up and leave the area when the latter peaked. But the people change more slowly. Joe, whose thick Italian accent clashed exuberantly with the Hong Kong–inflected phrasing of the previous owner, Bob's sister-in-law, whom we used to call The Otter (for her evident delight in all things, great or small), bustling here and there among the tables and then, in a single motion, back behind the counter, pouring the coffee, and calling out, "One BLT, white bread, toast, no butter," no more than a syllable or two ahead of him. Nathan, Tommy, Louie and the boys, with their leisurely two-hour breakfasts and the strict pecking order governing who sat at the main table and who was relegated to the periphery, all of them still keeping a hand in the real estate market and passing scurrilous judgements on children, though not as well on the grandchildren (who were, of course, instead to be pampered and pitied the shortcomings of their ungrateful parents). Mr. Jackman, who came in at nine and always sat alone, nodding shyly to the others, though never initiating it, and I used to wonder if he was okay, seeing how slowly he moved and how lonely he seemed, but the few times his daughter came in to have breakfast with him, she attacked him so viciously, and in public, he was almost in tears, and I thought, maybe it was nicer for him to be alone after all. Or Sophie and Rose, so cheerful all the time — Sophie the older, and Rose the quintessential "younger sister," still quiet and a bit demure, though both of them had long since married, had children, moved to Canada from England, lost husbands etc., and now they both were surely over seventy. The sort of sisters who are always Sophie-and-Rose, never Rose-and-Sophie.

But even these things change. One summer we returned from three months' travel and the feeling of the place had altered — Sophie seemed quieter than usual, and Rose no longer had her little smile. Only after a month or so, after once again settling into our place among the regulars, only then, one day having Sophie explain, while Rose sobbed quietly nearby, how her son had been among those gunned down in the shootings at Concordia that summer, something we'd heard about, though only in a general way, not understanding at the time, because we'd known them only by their first names, just how close it really was. That year was a sad year at the BP. And when we went away again the next spring, I remember Rose and Sophie coming up to my companion as we got our things together and were about to leave and giving her a little compact — "Something to remember us by," they said — completely ordinary, just a gesture really — of relief maybe, and of communal spirit. We'd been sitting at a table with the spring sun blazing in around us through the window — so bright I'd had to shield my eyes the whole time while I ate. Seeing them smile as they made that gesture, I felt as if, like King Canute, it might really be possible for someone to believe, if only for a moment, they could stop the tide. I could see them now, both as they were and, at the same time, standing on the village green in long white dresses in a long-since-vanished English countryside. And our travels that summer were exquisitely pleasant, and sometimes I would see my friend take out the compact, and we would briefly think of them — "the sisters," as we thought of them by then.

Now when I go in for breakfast, I feel a bit of a pang, and wonder about them, because they're never there. And although there's still that comfortable feeling of belonging, the acquaintanceships of such a place are tenuous, at best, so I don't know who might know what happened to them, or even if the answer would be one I'd want to hear.

And this, in some way, changes everything. As if a shadow had begun to fall across the village green, and time had started up again, and someone, roused out of their reverie (and without thinking), had begun once more the long walk back toward their former family home.

Throughout the city are numerous patches of unin-
tended wilderness. The stretch of abandoned railbed,
evidently still in private hands, behind the loft con-
version site on Castlefield. The steep slope along the
western edge of a nearby park, traversed diagonally
by a narrow footpath which, though overgrown in
summer, makes a pleasant shortcut to the subway.
The front yard of a tiny brick house down the street,
for sale for more than six months now, the state of
the yard mirroring, metaphorically, the state of the
sales process — the sequence of "For Sale" signs
marking a descent toward the ever-more-tolerant-
but-less-familiar realtors — whether the result of
tensions among the children who inherited it, or an
unwillingness by one, or all, to part, finally, with
what was once the family home.

Taking that path to the subway in early autumn,
it often strikes me that the steep, east-facing slope,
with its various wildflowers and tall, ungainly,
browning grasses, is the most beautiful of places in
this otherwise quite ordinary suburban park. Many,
it seems, agree, though last week a dissenting opinion
presented itself in the form of a city worker who, hav-
ing almost toppled from his ride-on mower, stood,
arms akimbo, at the base of the slope, cursing under
his breath and staring malevolently at the weedy
provocation. If beauty is in the eye of the beholder, so
too it seems is a certain vengeful theatricality which,

though the work itself may be wearing, provides at least a serviceable (if in the end no more than temporary) antidote.

Some years ago we moved into a house with friends, along that stretch of Harbord just west of Spadina. The neighbourhood consisted, then as now, of a friendly mix of restaurants, bookshops, bakeries and residences. Unlike most houses in the city, there was no front yard, only a sagging porch, built right to the footpath, in a quasi-European style, which, about-to-be-repaired for years, now tilted slightly to the southwest. In back, a long yard opened on the alley, with fences to the east and west, and between them our own patch of wilderness, colonized by feral cats. Along the fence between us and our neighbours to the west, a bed for growing basil and tomatoes in the summer had been cleared; the yard, apart from this, remained untended. Grapes, trained with great patience to create a block of shade beneath the trellis in our Italian neighbours' yard, had climbed the fence and into ours and, having made it there, gone wild, forming a tall, dense, tangled mass along the eastern boundary line. For much of our time there, an ancient MGB, weeds growing through its half-closed windows, occupied the middle of this yard. Bought in a fit of great enthusiasm by a younger brother flush with temporary cash, towed there with no doubt excellent intentions, "to be fixed up later," then sporadically forgotten as the cash and the enthusiasm — the one soon following the other — dissipated, it grew, in the course of the few years that followed, to resemble more and more a ruined temple, sinking slowly back into the jungle floor.

One day in early spring — our last spring, as it turned out, in that house — I'd been idling away the time, sipping at coffee that had now completely cooled, and looking out onto that patch of wilderness. A little snow still hung on by the fences and along the one side of the ruined car while elsewhere in the yard green had begun appearing everywhere. From the alleyway, an "older" woman, i.e., younger than I am now, looking first both ways, then entering the yard, approached the car and placed a burning joss stick on its roof. Clapping her hands together in the Buddhist style, she bowed once, and then lifted up her head. At once, like linked, multicoloured scarves pulled marvellously and without effort from a magician's previously empty fist, cat after cat leapt from the car's interior into the sudden light of that intensely green spring day.

Our teacher took us for a drive in the autumn hills. This was in the southern hemisphere, and as we began the climb toward the cooler suburbs, we could see, dotted here and there amidst the natives and varied evergreens, the liquidambars which had, brought down from the northern hemisphere, begun to turn, as always at this time of year — late March or early April — the lucent yellows, pumpkins, blood-reds and red-blacks these trees are prized for.

After a few kilometers we left the main road, several quick turns in succession bringing us out into the first of several leafy residential neighbourhoods, which rolled past, one after the other, just outside our window, merging seamlessly, alternating light and shadow all the while flashing hypnotically across the windscreen. As we drove, the sound of Mozart playing in the background made him hum, and every few blocks, pausing briefly, as if on some whim — though one conditioned by a larger, intimate familiarity — he'd turn again, and some new, slightly altered prospect would rise up before us. After some time driving in this fashion, we rounded a corner, coming suddenly upon a small house nestled on a slope not far from the Botanic Garden, surrounded on all sides by numerous camellia trees, several dozen overall, and of distinct varieties. This was his house. Many among the various camellias, he explained, were special to this place, hybrids developed by the man he'd bought it from, who'd lived for more than thirty years among them. Here and there the first few buds had just begun to open.

The front door opened on a quiet, ordered space, a short hall with a mat for outside shoes on one side and a closet on the other, beyond which an archway led off to the left into the sitting room and straight ahead the family room and kitchen could be seen. Taking our coats and bringing "inside slippers" from a back room, he made us tea, then showed us round the house. We saw stones, inkstones, books, photographs, the view from the study window. There were stones patterned with the two "belts" of Qing Dynasty officials; bars of stone as smooth and dense as milk chocolate; another, speckled with red, called "chicken's blood," that could be damaged by as little as a trace of acid from a fingertip. There were inksticks moulded with illustrations so sinuous and complex it would have been a shame to touch them with a brush. Traces of his father's world, his mother's world, the world he'd known when young.

At some point we set out walking through the winding streets of the neighbourhood, toward the local town. Once, he told us, walking near Hangzhou, he'd recognized the mushrooms described in old Daoist tales — and with a finger drew their contours in mid-air for us to see. Crows and kookaburras were calling overhead, and magpies carolled at us from the lawns. Stopping a moment, he inclined his head toward them, adding that, in China, magpies — not precisely these, perhaps, but if not, certainly their

cousins — were called *xique*, literally "happy bird."
And with this we were off again, eventually reaching
the center of town, where the liquidambars, lining
the main street, were at their absolute peak. Choos-
ing a sidewalk café whose tables looked out on this
blaze of colour, we passed a pleasant hour or so and,
after lunch, meandered back through the burgeoning
warmth of the autumn afternoon.

At home again, he made more tea and, getting
us settled, disappeared once more into the back, re-
turning this time with an armful of small spiral note-
books, which he dropped onto the couch between us.

These had been composed during a time when
the country stood still, doors and windows taped over
as though for a storm that was passing, but whose
end was not in sight. Considering their background,
he believed, the family had been lucky. Though the
Red Guards had come often, they had, having sealed
the entrance to the library that first night, afterwards
appeared content to trash the contents of the other
rooms, and leave again. The family, over time, had
grown almost accustomed to this new, peculiar
rhythm, and soon ceased to tidy up after each visit,
leaving the various belongings strewn across the

floors — and after this the visits became shorter, fi-
nally (though never without terror) near-perfunctory.
It was during this time, having begun to navigate the
scattered objects underfoot almost without thinking,
that he'd started writing out his own translations —
Keats and Shelley first, then later any poet, known
or unknown, any poem, of whatever period or pur-
pose — in these notebooks small enough to fit into
the palm of a hand, each neatly preserved now in a
plastic sleeve, and without, so far as we could see, a
single crossing-out or erasure.

Such an act, in those days, if discovered, could
have seen him beaten, publicly humiliated — depend-
ing on the circumstances, even killed. Yet, like the
others in his family, it had seemed to him that he
was simply going on, following the path of least (or
possibly, more to the point, not totally expunged)
resistance. If a book was needed from the library, well
then the hinges of the door to the library could be re-
moved, albeit taking care to leave the tape that sealed
the other side intact. And when the book was finished,
then the process could be just as easily reversed.

All learning, our teacher said once, grows out
of this need to cope. Thinking back now, I remember
our class repeating after him, practicing each new
phrase, the sound unruly as the off-key squawking
of young magpies responding to a parent's song. Our
teacher is the sort of person who might come upon
the mushrooms of immortality and decline to taste
them, who looks after his parents and lives alone
in the hills. Amid the eccentric music of birds, he

devotes himself to the classical music of Europe. I often think of the things we saw that day. Stones, inkstones, books, photographs. The kookaburras, whose cry makes us laugh. Longjing tea, which we tasted there for the first time. "This tea is too old," he told us, pouring water over the leaves, "though if you like the taste please take it," and handed us the package. Like anyone else, he is simply himself. As for those beautiful inksticks, whatever might have been written with their ink will never be written now. "But you," he continued, turning toward us, kettle in hand, "are from Canada: to have brought you here to see the autumn leaves is like playing with the axe in front of the master carpenter! *Ban men nong fu!*"

Ban men nong fu, I find myself repeating. But what sort of door would it be then, I wonder, gracing this Master Ban's house? For some reason I picture an iconic late-afternoon scene, the house in a clearing in an otherwise heavily wooded region, sunlight filtering down into the understory, making everything glow with a strangely beautiful yellowy-green colour, like that by which, according to the guidebooks, true Longjing tea can be distinguished.

Ban men nong fu.

The phrase, expressing mild approbation, leavened with a suitable bemusement, is derived from the last line of a Ming Dynasty poem. It alludes to an old story, while at the same time reflecting on its writer. The poet, a certain Ming Dynasty gentleman, coming on the site of Li Bai's grave and finding bits of poetry scrawled everywhere around it, much of it of dubious quality, nonetheless feels compelled to add his own, by way of commentary. With poetry, it would seem, as with Longjing tea, it is the colour, fineness, and other such tangible yet ephemeral qualities that distinguish the real thing from the various imitations on offer along the road — whether the road be one leading to the grave of a famous poet, or one taken up entirely with selling tea.

It was some years later that we visited the town of Longjing for ourselves. It lies in the hills not far from Hangzhou, our teacher's ancestral home. We'd gone by local bus, which, by the time we boarded it, was packed with foreign and domestic tourists — so much so that, finding my glasses knocked askew at some point in the crush, I'd had to snake an arm up, bending the hand down awkwardly, like a flamingo's head beside my own, to rescue them — only to discover that in the course of these contortions, one of the small screws holding them together had been lost, rendering them quite useless after that. Arriving at the stop for the Tea Museum, most of the passengers disembarked, a certain cooperative ambiguity in the driver's announcement having suggested that the Dragon Well, or *long jing*, was to be found here. In fact the Tea Museum is a recent innovation, set up at some distance from the eponymous well, and the dragon once said to reside there and control the rains. A few more minutes brought us to the last stop on the route, at the edges of the village proper.

Following the cognoscenti, we soon found ourselves walking along the main street of the village, which was lined with houses, each intent on selling tea. A rickety table, half in shade, stood on the porch of each. Here freshly roasted leaves, on small white plates, were set out on display, and family members offered sample cups at prices somehow not in keeping with the rustic scene. A woman, evidently local, who'd attached herself in conversation to another party on the bus, having delivered them to the front porch of a small house, now detached herself and came toward us.

"You're from America," she stated. "Buying tea today." Which, finding us from Canada, proved less effective as an opening than she'd anticipated. Undaunted, she continued, arguing that we could sightsee later, that the tea was famous, finally declaring in frustration, somewhat enigmatically, gesturing dismissively in the direction we were headed, "That teahouse is for tourist, more expensive!"

After a while we passed the complex which surrounds the Dragon Well. Several tour buses sat waiting in the shade. By now the crowds were thinning out, the end of the village was in sight. As we approached, a woman on a front porch looked up from her work and waved for us to join her. *"Lai, lai!"* she insisted, as we kept on walking, promising to stop back later, finally calling after us, "If you go that way you'll never return!" But by now we were following an old stone road, which in turn followed a stream, through a landscape of hills dotted with dark green glossy tea plants.

The road, indeed, seemed intent on leading us farther and farther from the town. As tea plantations gave way to trees and gentle unkempt countryside, here or there a tumbledown house would appear, half-hidden behind a wall, or the occasional small business selling drinks or food. At length, passing one of these establishments, we happened on a group of students. At a table set right into the midst of the stream, they sat laughing and eating together, bare feet in the cool water on such a hot day. These students, too, I found myself thinking, are like the *xique* — the magpies, or "happy birds" — laughing and talking amongst themselves, then seeing us, turning to wave so joyously.

A few summers ago we were staying in a second-storey room in a long, low, sixties-style building among other buildings of a similar vintage, most of them sorority or fraternity houses, not far from the university gates. The singing and laughing and drinking sessions would begin around midnight and come to their natural end just before dawn. Because of all the noise and shouting it was hard to sleep, and because I'd just hurt my back, and it was difficult to move around, I'd often spend the afternoon lying down gazing out the window, or else turning the pages of some book.

The room contained a desk, two armchairs, a small kitchen table and chairs, two bedside tables and a bed. By day I thought of the bed as a daybed, and lay there looking out at the deepening green and gold of the pines. Around 2 or 3 p.m. a cloud of white moths would appear, spiralling among the boughs, and from time to time, bushy tail held straight back, a squirrel would materialize, lolloping across a twist of phone line, or hanging briefly upside down from a bough, face in the pine needles, eating something small and delicious.

"*Songshu* in the *songshu*," remarked a young friend some months later. "Pine mice in the pine trees." By then we were back home in Toronto, and our young friend, on loan to us from his home city of Wuhan, was standing in the dining room looking

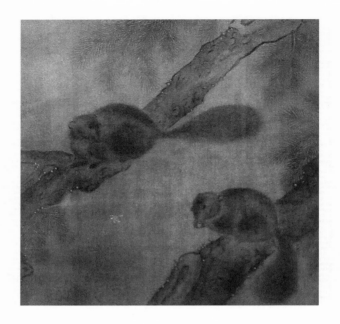

at an old print on the wall, of some Chinese squirrels among the Chinese pines. Once he's finished with his studies, perhaps he'll go back home, get married, live the kind of life we can all imagine for him. Or maybe he'll remain among the big cities of the West, gradually becoming lost to that life, which would have been his had he never set out for this place, where all too many doors, it seems, are already open to him.

My back, by this time, was much better. The cedar tree out front as well, which had nearly died in our absence. This according to our neighbour, who'd watered it — watered it so well, in fact, that by now it's grown higher than our house, and thrust its roots so deeply it carries our house on its toes. In just this way many a child, placing one foot, then the other, atop a willing adult's feet, has been walked across the rooms of a remembered childhood home.

The squirrels who spend time on our roof never tire of defending the house from those of us who live inside it. They leave zippered tracks in the backyard grass, use the neighbourhood power lines as highways, and on frigid winter afternoons take their stand on the study windowsill unafraid, glaring in with a peculiar ire and eating mouthful after mouthful of snow. Come spring they'll stretch themselves full-length again along the young cherry boughs, devouring as many buds as possible before they blossom. And yet of all the harm that is done in this world, they do so very little of it after all, dropping a bagel half or not-yet-fully-opened peanut on the way to their outposts in the Manitoba maples.

I came upon one of these squirrels some weeks ago, during the worst of the recent heat waves. It lay prostrate on the sill outside the kitchen window, nearly blind with thirst, its little heart pumping. "Me too," our glances seemed to say as we looked at one another through the glass, and since then I can no longer find it in myself to raise my voice when it or its companions come around.

The Manitoba maples, or "trees of heaven" as they're known locally, are another story. They sprout amidst all my neighbour's careful plantings, crowd out even the oaks and wild sumac, and push their way through the least crack in the concrete steps, where I pull them out by the handful whenever I come across them.

As for our friend from Wuhan, he went home for the summer, and hasn't been heard from since.

Squirrels, friends, the trees of heaven — in a world as wide as this, maybe it's okay to navigate by these few stars.

One day, walking by the Torrens, I met a man. He was coming toward me along the path, and when we were close enough to speak, he stopped, setting down in the grass near his feet a small plastic bag he was carrying. He took a moment to clear his throat, and then, in what was clearly his best English, asked whether this was the way to the park.

There are many parks in and around the city of Adelaide, and we were at that moment standing in one of them. He had a street map, he told me (was this what was in the small bag?), but had chanced upon the river, and now, as it gradually became clear, he wanted to know whether one could reach the city center by following the course of the river rather than the roads.

One could. He had only to avoid crossing any bridges to the other side, then turn left through the university. . . . We were already nodding our good-byes when it occurred to me to ask whether he spoke *zhongwen*, by which of course I meant what we call Mandarin.

At once we were on another footing; there was much to discuss. He'd arrived just the day before, and today (being Monday) the friend he was visiting had gone to work, so he'd set out to see the city on his own. That the first person he'd met could speak his own language, that both of us had chosen to walk by the river from which neither of us wished to depart

. . . We conducted ourselves word by word, phrase by phrase, making our way back and forth between English and Mandarin largely by guesswork. He appeared to be a little older than I was, possibly in his sixties. This was, I explained, my last day to walk by the river, as the next day we would be leaving for Queensland, then Canada. . . .

No matter! he said, and wrote out his name and address on a scrap of paper. He'd retired to Tasmania for the beautiful view — and indeed the address he wrote down was a number along View Street. Our meeting, he continued, was *yuanfen*: if you move you must write to me from the new address, if I move I must do the same. People are busy with their own lives, he told me, it doesn't matter if ten or twenty years pass, we can still meet — and next time my English and your Mandarin will both be perfect!

Passing-Cloud Lin, I thought of him for a time, until I was able to consult a better dictionary. Surpassing Clouds, his name seemed to be, Cloud-Transcending Lin.

The feeling of that meeting fades a little each day, though the slight inaudible grinding sensation of the clouds as they pass one another overhead still reminds me of him. And the scrap of paper remains tucked in my wallet, teaching me very slowly, I think, how to live in retirement in the world. *Yuanfen?* I looked it up in the dictionary. It means: predestined affinity, Buddhist fate.

When the first loneliness of autumn strikes, I think of my friend Liu. The maples turn bronze, the wind rounds a corner a little too quickly, it's nearly time for classes to start, but my friend is no longer here.

Opening my lesson book, I think of him. Did a whole country — could a whole country's history have made this Liu whom I call my friend?

One could ask: what is friendship? What is there to miss in a friend? The threesome taking turns waltzing in pairs in the Summer Palace, above the dust and smoke, at the top of Longevity Hill. The old emperors would be envious, if they weren't just bodies without heads, sacks of cloth and folded feet. Like the Thousand Buddhas, who have vandals to thank for their final enlightenment, whose minds have joined the void.

My lesson book says "It's been a long time since you've seen your mother, and there are many things you'd like to say to her." True. When a parent dies it's the strangest feeling: never again will anyone care to know where you are on this earth.

And then there is friendship.

One could say: when a smile slices into you. When a conversation takes years, among people who haven't yet learned to hide their happiness.

If I could find that feeling in a lesson book, I'd study that much harder, or perhaps just more slowly.

When will I see that smile again?

哪辈子再看到那个微笑?

I write this walking the blue pathways after rain, between cricket hill and cicada grove.

YUANMING YUAN:
THE GARDEN OF PERFECT BRIGHTNESS

On or about the first official day of summer, as the year begins to heat up, I go rummaging once again in the box in which seldom-used linens are stored, looking for a certain remnant of raw silk left over from a set of curtains which have long since rotted and fallen to pieces. This remnant, little-used and hence preserved, is still in good shape after fifty years, and when hung in the small south window, not only helps to blunt the summer heat but surprises the midday sun, as it turns the corner of the house, with a sudden grove of stylized bamboo: brown and green and gold, with a few blackened leaf tips representing the deepest shade. At once the onlooker feels cooled, as if by a breeze rushing through real bamboo, and the mind begins to wander in that illumined square, endlessly generating the scenes of former travels, relics as apparently solid as the combs of hand-carved bamboo or, later, moulded plastic, incised with the names of the hotels that once provided them, as a matter of course and unremarkable token of courtesy, to their guests. At the end of summer the square of silk with its magic-lantern scenery will be folded away once more in its box, where it will lie dormant over the winter. One day even this piece of silk, like all old silk, will cease to be, descending into various desiccated shreds, and the compulsion to remember, as if this were some alchemy whereby experience might be sorted into dross and gold, will fade away.

In the northeast corner of the grounds of Yuanming Yuan, the site of the former residence of the old Qing emperors, known in English as the Old Summer Palace, lie the ruins of the "Western Mansions," a complex of eighteenth-century Italianate buildings designed for the Qianlong emperor by two Jesuit priests, one French and one Italian, then resident in the Qianlong court. Though representing only a small part of the grounds of Yuanming Yuan, the Western Mansions area contained not only the buildings themselves, many constructed of marble, and filled with European art and furnishings, but also various fountains and monuments, in addition to a large maze, built in a style then popular in Europe. Along with most of the rest of Yuanming Yuan, these structures were pulled down, burned and looted, first by the French and British forces during the Second Opium War, then later, more extensively, in 1900, by the Eight-Power Expeditionary Force during its occupation of Beijing. Because of the marble used in their construction, the ruins of the Western Mansions buildings (if not the buildings proper) have managed to survive. This was not true of the structures in the rest of Yuanming Yuan and, over the many decades following, a number of small farms and villages grew up to take their place. For much of the eighties and early nineties, the site was home to a growing community of independent, hence dissident, artists, filmmakers, and writers. This community was largely ignored by the authorities until some of the artists began to garner international attention, at which point it was finally dispersed. Since then, many of the "natural" features of the grounds have been restored, and it is possible to stroll the maze again and, on finally reaching its center, climb the restored tower once used by the emperor to look down on his servants blundering from one dead-end passage to another. Despite the ruins' historical significance, and the numerous visitors who come as a result, the site is large, and often feels still strangely half-abandoned. It is seen as a place to come and stroll in peace, far from the bustle of the city. If you come, there is a grove of bamboo at one end of the lake not far from the ruins of the Western Mansions. On a hot summer day, the leaves there hang down almost motionless, despite the breeze that rises on occasion from the lake, so still they might be something printed on old silk and hung up in the small south-facing window of a house in some far-distant foreign city. It is possible to walk the full circumference of this lake. The path is well tended, and you may pass and nod there to those seen earlier among the ruins, assimilating into memory what then seems of interest, amidst the interference of short bursts of static from the rusted speakers set high on the lampposts and the faint strains of a music rising as if from the ground itself, which turns out to be coming from a few strange rock-shaped speakers set along the edges of the path.

The couple from Chicago are Christians (so they inform us at the first, unlikely, moment) and are on their honeymoon. Asked "Why Shanghai?" they explain they prayed to God, and this is where he sent them.

Shanghai is a city of thirteen million people, eight million bicycles, numerous factories, and an uncountable number of mosquitoes. At night the floor attendant comes with an old-fashioned hand pump filled with perfumed insecticide to spray the curtains of our room. During the day, the sky registers the browns and yellow-browns of airborne soots and catalytic toxins, nitrous oxides, low ominous smokes that hover over the "ancient waterways," modern streets, and what I suppose must be the blocks referred to in the Western media as grey, Stalinist architecture (though they resemble, in essence, blocks of similar form and function all across America). The water in the ditches, sometimes, runs with dye.

People from Shanghai are quick to say to visitors, when complimented on the energy of the city, "But the air's not too good," or "Yes, but the water's awful." As for the "toiling masses" expected by many first-time visitors, in fact the people are by and large extremely friendly, clean, neatly dressed, and apparently quite happy, happier than one would think a similar crowd in Europe, or North America.

Still, unhappiness is unhappiness. The couple from Chicago attend services at Shanghai's single visible cathedral, placed high up in a separate, balcony section with an interpreter while the locals crowd the ground floor, overflow the room, and spill over into several adjacent rooms where the sermon is broadcast over loudspeakers. The couple from Chicago note the attentiveness of the crowd and are much impressed by both their own treatment and the threatening (admonitional?) nature of the sermon, as they understand it, in translation.

Although it is their honeymoon, the new-born husband is quick to expound on how the love of God is the only important love. Everything else is secondary, he says. This probably does not bode well for their future life together.

And it is true, they do not appear that happy here. Thinking of God, I think of childhood, and endless floating-dreams. Of being able to do *impossible* things. Maybe this is because of the acrobats. The stage is harshly lit and up there they spin, balance, juggle, fly through the air and amaze us. Perhaps these too are gods, if of a minor sort. But *tutelary* gods, so light and agile it seems they never need to touch the ground — or needing to, if momentarily, are nonetheless immune to its trials and sorrows.

We stayed in a certain guesthouse for six weeks one autumn on the grounds of a large research institute in the far west of Beijing. Our window looked out from the third floor of the building, and directly out this window could be seen the brittle oval leaves and ripening fruits of two flourishing persimmon trees, as well as the elegant long-tailed magpies that came, more of them each day, to peck beak-shaped holes in the orange flesh of the persimmons and exult in their spicy sweetness.

The western parts of Beijing are not generally so well known for their cuisine as are their eastern counterparts. Whatever lowered expectations we may have had as a result were, however, soon dispelled, beginning the day of our arrival, when one of our hosts introduced us to a bustling two-storey establishment specializing entirely in mushroom soups. Let me begin by saying that Beijing mushroom soup bears no relation to the whitish, vaguely mushroom-flavoured liquids, concocted of sturdy jiggling cylinders of unknown provenance dumped out of cans and into pots of milk or water, that we, along with countless other North American children, grew up with in the fifties. On a burner in the center of the table, simmering away, was a large pot, into which an entire plucked and gutted rooster, complete with red cockscomb, had been placed. To this were to be added vegetables of our choice, along with any of the thirty or more varieties of mushrooms depicted in the photographs that decorated the four walls, mushrooms in a bewildering array of fanciful shapes: some compact as miniature steamed buns or small dolls' hats, others frilled or branching like specimens of some tropical coral or seaweed, still others chunky, massive, and dense, shaped randomly or misshapen, as chance would have it.

Within the next few days we found, in quick succession, two more restaurants in the neighbourhood. The first, a branch of the famous roast-duck restaurant Quan Ju De, was right next to the mushroom restaurant, while the second, Ying Fu Lou, or Overflowing Fortune/Luck, which soon became our favourite, was across the street, inside the entrance to an older residential compound. The Ying Fu Lou turned out to offer a range of possibilities, from superb renditions of traditional everyday Beijing dishes (chicken fired with chiles and peanuts, shredded pork with variegated peppers and bamboo, sweet corn with gourd and pine nuts) to banquet fare (whole lambs' legs roasted in cumin, sun-dried abalone braised in wine, asparagus spears in garlic sauce). All this served up by a staff drawn from every part of the country, and together representing, we were told, the full range of regional nationalities. Many fine teas were also to be had, and we soon became habituated to our pot of palest, fresh green Longjing tea, ordered almost before our seating was completed, savouring the unexpected sweetness rising from that first slight bitterness, as we debated and dithered our way once more through the menu. Each day we would discuss trying a different restaurant that evening, but then each night, as dusk fell, we would find ourselves drawn back again, drawn back with an attraction as fierce as that exerted on the magpies by the ripening persimmons.

If the western part of Beijing is not as widely known as it could be for its restaurants, it is for its parks, including one, Badachu, or Eight Grand Places, particularly renowned for its autumn colours.

Among stands of brilliant reddening and yellowing trees can still be found a few endlessly tumbledown, endlessly repaired buildings, some of them small temples, others former residences of well-known by-gone figures, scattered among the numerous slippery paths leading uphill toward viewpoints long recommended by tradition and now partially occluded, whether by foliage, smog, or a wavering certainty as to what exactly, nowadays, should most command the visitor's attention. It might come as something of a surprise, then, in the midst of such serious, if nebulous, historical considerations, to suddenly notice a pair of white paws or a careless tail extending from beneath the shrubbery at one's feet, and there, pushing aside the foliage, to find a cat, perhaps with several kittens.

There is a saying in China that goes something along the lines of "Black cat, white cat — what's the difference? Whatever catches mice, that's a good cat." It's attributed to Deng Xiaoping, and because of historical circumstances, has particularly strong political implications. In English we might say that the ends justify the means, though whether the two sayings would then be equivalent or incommensurate, I have no way of discovering. What I do know is that in the parks of Beijing the population of cats — black cats, calico, and especially the multitudes of white cats (many of them congenitally deaf) — is an explosion no longer imminent but already at hand, as my friend and I quickly discovered on our arrival at Badachu. We'd just turned right past a topiary version of the Olympic mascot family and begun to make our way uphill when, around a bend in the path, partially obscured by trees, we happened upon a half-dozen or so young uniformed soldiers, both men and women, all of them crouched or stretched out amidst the shrubbery, playing with an extended family of cats and their brood. One young soldier was stroking a tiny white kitten on a khaki lap while another trailed a stick to be chased in the dust. Yet another squatted down dangling a morsel of food while still others took care to refill the cache of plastic dishes hidden there with tidbits from their own provisions, or else water from the plastic water bottles being sold throughout the park. All the while the cats jumped and played, curled their tails and purred, cats and soldiers utterly taken up with one another. For these particular cats, I couldn't help thinking, the necessity of catching mice in order to be thought a "good cat" was long past.

Toward the end of our stay that autumn we were invited, along with several dozen other visitors, to a celebratory banquet in one of the nearby upscale restaurants, located on the top floor of one of the brand-new shopping towers in a modernized mini-business-district that had sprung up within easy walking distance of the several major universities that occupy an extensive area of northwest Beijing, not far from Yuanming Yuan, the grounds of the former Qing emperor's palace, destroyed during the Opium Wars by the French and British and since that time left in its ruined state. One whole side of the restaurant had been taken over for the function and, arriving somewhat late, we were guided toward a table in the midst of the group. My friend sat to my left, while directly to my right was a man we'd both met a number of times over the previous twenty years, always in an amiable setting, and at locations scattered variously around the world, and so knew reasonably well, in the way that one knows someone one has met from time to time in places that are home to neither, after travelling some distance, and at some not inconsiderable cost. Several of these times had been in China, where he'd taken up, as is the Chinese way, the role of local host, honoured to be entertaining foreign visitors and friends. Tonight, though, others played this role, including him among the honoured guests.

Over the course of the evening, course after course continued to arrive, be sampled, and eventually return whence it had come. Massive boat-shaped platters of sushi, plates full of delicately seasoned shrimp, miniature crabs or scallops, sliced duck with a pinkish flavoured salt in small bowls on the side, chicken served with vinegar and ginger, doufu (steamed and fried), braised bitter melon, eel cooked in the Shanghai style, along with various other dishes I can no longer call to mind. On the other side of our acquaintance, seated to his right, was another older, white-haired, man. In the midst of all the comings and goings, I began to notice them talking animatedly and toasting one another, over and over, with small glasses of *baijiu*, both downing them in one go, laughing in a progressively happier, progressively louder, manner as the night wore on. This was something I'd never seen before in our more than twenty years' acquaintance with this man, who'd always seemed, though friendly, still a bit reserved, though open, still quite proper, even circumspect. Turning and pouring me a glass for good measure, he introduced his white-haired friend, bringing me into the midst of their ongoing reminiscence. Many years ago, it turned out, they'd been at university together, one of the prestigious ones nearby in fact, when (here a toast) "certain historical changes occurred, disrupting all previous plans." They'd entered in 1954 and so been partway through their studies at the start of the Hundred Flowers Campaign. Initially there'd been great ferment and excitement on the campuses, and both of them had taken part. The first denunciations, followed by arrests, had come as a surprise, but most of their classmates had soon sensed in what direction the prevailing winds were blowing now, and hunkered down into a cowed, internally contained resentful silence. Only a few, these two among them, had felt the need to speak out, even in that climate. Not that they'd been unaware, by then, of the potential dangers, they insisted, though perhaps (another toast) a bit naive about the full extent of what the consequences might turn out to be. The result was that, for the next decade, each was forced to eke out an existence working on the land while famine swirled on every side, living among peasants who, though they might share the hardships of that life, remained wary of such city folk who'd come to them with obviously dangerous political associations. With that, and then the lost years of the Cultural Revolution, it had been five decades till they'd met again. If in a human life there are sometimes clouds, and at others a "hiddenness" that's hard to penetrate, there are, too, moments when a man's true character blazes forth, illumining the life that formed it as brightly as any sun. "Just *look* at this!" he said, raising his glass in pure amazement with the one hand, while gesturing casually about him with the other, indicating not just ours and all the other tables, spread from edge to edge with foods of all descriptions, but the life that we were living now — which seemed to most of us, the young and foreigners, so ordinary, and so natural.

A few days later I returned to our room in the guesthouse in the afternoon and, as had become my habit, went immediately to the window. There, amidst the leaves of the persimmons, were a dozen or so young uniformed soldiers, one or two of them on ladders nearly at eye level, others waiting below, catching the fruits as they were tossed, all with much glee and larking about, from those in the heavens, as it were, to those still back on earth, filling sack after sack from just the two trees. The magpies, as beautiful in life as in a Song Dynasty painting, were nowhere to be seen. Once the last persimmon had been picked, the troops moved off, still grinning boyishly with the pleasure of the afternoon's assignment, carrying the sacks and ladders off to some unknown location, leaving the trees stripped bare as dusk began to fall.

Quite often, I'll admit, curiosity gets the better of me, and the consequences, or their absence, are rarely predictable. Before we left, I asked someone I'd picked out for her kind face as likely to be approachable on the subject, what would have become of the persimmons. She said she hadn't known anything about those trees, as her office was in another building in the institute and she'd had no cause to visit the guesthouse thus far, but lately she'd noticed persimmons cropping up on the desks of several administrative higher-ups in the buildings she frequented. The numbers on these desks had been gradually decreasing as the days went by.

I can picture this scene, perhaps more clearly now for never having seen it in reality: persimmons aglow on the cold desks in those deserted offices at the end of the day, once everyone has gone home, and the first dogs have been brought out for exercise, and the magpies have returned to the persimmon trees, weaving their shadows among the emptied branches, and, it being almost dinnertime, we've started to think again of Longjing tea, and made our way back to the Ying Fu Lou.

Spring has come late to the city this year. The new leaves, usually so quick to go from bud to summer green, have opened slowly and, for weeks, their new green, not quite strong enough to hide the branches, has been glowing all along the street. In the backyard the neighbour's cherry tree has held its blossoms longer than on previous occasions, and the squirrels, like all true connoisseurs, content with not just what is finest but evidently, even more, with what is most remote, have stretched themselves in graceful arcs out and along the farthest and most inaccessible of all its swaying, perfumed, outer branches.

The yard is home to numerous half-wild, half-domesticated cats. This is their neighbourhood. They criss-cross its expanse, and have made small tunnels under two of the fences, just large enough for one cat to pass through at a time, facilitating their roaming from place to place in search of food, or sun — or a shady place to lie down and drift, all the while with one eye half-open, watching for others of their kind. In years past, kittens would be born beneath the front steps of the house, but the neighbour, saddened by the death of even one among them, gathered the females one by one and had them spayed. I'd thought we'd see no more of the small black and small brindled adolescents practicing their skills with moths and dandelion heads, but this spring two more brindleds have appeared, through what means who can say?

As the city ages, so the yard ages. The tall, spreading sumac in the far back corner has died, whether of disease or through the machinations of the other neighbour, who always complained it stained her laundry (by way of the birds, who ate its seeds each fall), and the wildflowers on the overgrown slope have themselves been overtaken by tall grasses with feathery seedheads, which wave slightly in the breeze, and incline me to indolence.

But some things are unchanged, or else have truly prospered: the dandelions, which have taken over much of the northern side, along the fence, and the irises, which, like the cats, have made their way under the fence and line its southern side. I too have aged, and love the irises and dandelions when they are in bloom, and the lilac, which, for a few weeks on end, fills the dining room with its scent.

All spring I've watched the cats and kittens in the morning, stalking birds. This year it seems that fewer of the small birds have returned to the gardens, though some are still to be found in the ravine nearby. Instead, we hear the sound of crows, and see the cats, when they stalk them, doing so with caution.

Since turning fifty I too, it seems, am no longer able to catch birds. Instead I watch the clouds, and stretch out in the sun all day. Now and then there is the hum of bees and, when the wind is right, the scent of mint and clover, and today at last I see my alter ego — that old black and white cat we once took for dead — is back, curled up after a few days' absence (who can say whether asleep or not) there in the shade beneath the lilacs.

A child is given the role of a buttercup in the school play, standing in her stiff yellow costume beside the other buttercups. Then there is a poem about buttercups. Much later, another:

> Buttercup
> held up to the chin — this mirror
> from childhood.

This means that if, catching the sun, the glossy petals reflect a patch of yellow light onto the skin it is a true buttercup, otherwise it is just another yellow flower. A poem exerts a subtle pressure, like the sayings memorized in childhood, "Step on a crack — break your mother's back," the logical underpinnings of which we hoped to grasp one day when we were older, though by the time we were older we had somehow forgotten all about it. Such old sayings and folk tales drift across the earth, severed from their roots. Few people can distinguish a buttercup root from any other; most roots are moist and white, or dun-coloured, or rose-sheathed, and in any case we recognize things principally by their flowers or fruits. Only a few experts, and the kinds of animals that burrow underground, would be aware of the differences. The child who plays a buttercup in the school pageant is the woman who dies, having remembered this moment all her life, and thus we are moved to compassion. Compassion resides in the wrists, along with an immediate desire to help others.

There is only one whose entire person is as sturdy and graceful as a wrist. It is Guanyin. A statue of Guanyin stands beside the house that has been turned into a temple in her honour. She is the sort of person to remain untroubled by the knowledge that she is merely a statue of herself. Tall and white, she is like a root or a wrist, both a god and an oversized doll. Even if she were able to stoop down and look into the windows of her house, she would still be too big to go in. Three pine trees grow nearby on the adjacent property, still healthy, but bent nearly perpendicular, as though a strong west wind were blowing perpetually. Actually the wind doesn't blow for long on any given day, though the grit flies whenever a bus passes.

Much of this part of the city has been levelled bit by bit. Rebuilt with multi-use concrete buildings, it is nonetheless home to a few startling signs:

— Celestial Travel —

Grocery Convenience:
— Spanish, Italian, Philippino and Asian Foods —

Supermercado:
— African, Canadian, East & West Indian —
Newfoundland, Spanish

Most of us here are fairly recent immigrants from one place or another, Guanyin too. I think of her as the queen of the northwest part of the city. First I watch for those bent pines, and then she is there, her pure whiteness neither that of concrete nor of marble, standing beside her house. It's just about the last nice old house along this stretch of Keele, for as far as the eye can see.

LU XUN'S DESK

One August morning, a friend and I set out to find
a certain small museum dedicated to the twentieth-
century Chinese writer Lu Xun. The museum was
said to be located in the Fuchengmennei district —
not far from the neighbourhood where we were stay-
ing — in the grounds of the courtyard-style house in
the northwest quarter of the old city where Lu Xun
lived during the latter part of his Beijing years. Leav-
ing the Fuchengmen stop on the subway, we set out
in what from our map appeared to be the right direc-
tion, entering a neighbourhood of narrow laneways,
which ran off irregularly, branching from time to
time in some more promising direction which itself
would, without warning, turn, or branch, or bring
us finally, after some time, to another dead end well
short of our destination. Trudging along, we might
find someone glancing up, surprised to see us there,
or sense the odd look of suspicion, but for the most
part our presence went unremarked. Children ran
from house to house, or flowed around the groups
of old men gathered playing cards or chess, while
women hung out laundry by the front doors. Now
and then we'd stop to ask for help, another halting
conversation yielding yet another arm gesturing in
yet another general direction, the sequence of arms,
as we made our way around the neighbourhood,
gradually filling out the spokes of an irregular wheel,
at the center of which (presumably) lay our intended

destination — what the locals, in responding to our questions, spoke of, not as the museum, but as "Lu Xun's former residence." The morning air was hot already, laden with the dust of the northern desert, which in summer settles lacelike over everything, and as we walked, the hypnotic heat of the season rising degree by degree, moments, traces from his works — often little more than a taste or colour, fiery and insubstantial as a whiff of Shaoxing wine — kept coming back to me. It took us close to an hour, retracing our steps this way and that within the maze of laneways, to locate the right street and, at last, only a few blocks from the subway as it turned out, the museum. Set back from the street, behind the main wall of the compound, it at first seemed simply one more of the many buildings housing government departments we'd seen scattered through the city. Only on finding, through the main gate, raised up on a pedestal and staring back at us, the bust of Lu Xun, circa 1933, resembling (incongruously) a younger Stalin, did we realize we had arrived.

Lu Xun was thirty when he first came to Beijing. This was in May of 1912, a little more than half a year after the fall of the Qing Dynasty and the founding of the Republic of China, and a year and a half after his return to Shaoxing, following nearly a decade in Japan. Earlier, in February of the same year, impatient for change and disillusioned with local politics, fed up with the corruption that had firmly re-established itself in the wake of the revolution, he'd resigned his post as headmaster and teacher of natural sciences and physiology at the local Normal School, and, at the invitation of the then Minister, taken up a position in the Department of Education of the new republic, moving first to Nanjing, then, when the Ministry was relocated from the southern to the northern capital, Beijing. While in Shaoxing he'd lived, much as he had while growing up, in the largest of the three family compounds in the southern part of the city, sharing it, as was customary for the period, with close relations from several branches of the clan, and living under the same roof as, not just his mother, but also, for the first time since their marriage four years previous, the village wife, Zhu An, she'd chosen for him. Of this wife, he said once later, "This was a gift my mother gave me. I had no choice but to accept it and provide for her. As for love, this was something I knew nothing of." Now, preparing to start a new life, leaving Shaoxing behind, he travelled north alone.

Lu Xun would live for fourteen years, in total, in Beijing. For the first seven he stayed, as he had on his arrival in the city, in the Shaoxing Hostel, with others from his region. It was not until 1919, in the middle of December, that he made the journey back. This was to be the last time he would set foot in Shaoxing. Returning to Beijing, he brought with him his mother and Zhu An, installing them in the house on Badaowan he'd bought that fall, just before setting out. A not dissimilar journey is recounted at the beginning of the story "My Old Home," whose narrator, "braving the bitter cold," has come back from an unnamed distant city to the hometown he left twenty years before. The house the clan has lived in has been sold and is to change hands by the year's end, and the narrator, somewhat reluctantly it seems, has come back — as he says, "this time without illusions" — to see to the selling of those furnishings that must be left behind, say his goodbyes and, in the two weeks left till New Year's Day, make arrangements for what family remains — his mother and his nephew Hong'er — to accompany him on his return.

While the main theme of "My Old Home" might be said to be the idea of hope, the story, nonetheless, is permeated with a sense of home and homelessness, and has always called to mind our first Chinese teacher, Shu-Ying Tsau. Shu-Ying had grown up in Xiangshan, the Fragrant Hills, outside Beijing, and by the time we met, her childhood home, in some way never fully explicated, no longer existed there. It was in Shu-Ying's classes that we first met Lu Xun's work, making our way slowly, vocabulary list in hand, through "The Comedy of the Ducks," the short, oddly charmed recollection of the blind Russian poet Eroshenko, who stayed with the family for much of the year, beginning in the spring of 1922.

"The Comedy of the Ducks," like "My Old Home" before it, was written in the house on Badaowan. A lively, if at times contentious, atmosphere prevailed there, both younger brothers and their families having, by then, moved into the compound. In the preface to *A Call to Arms*, the collection in which both "My Old Home" and "The Comedy of the Ducks" appear, Lu Xun writes of his time before this, in the Shaoxing Hostel. On the eastern side of the hostel was a three-room studio, and in the courtyard of this studio, a scholar tree, from which, so it was said, a young girl, some time in the past, had hanged herself. Though the tree had grown taller now, so tall that its branches were out of reach, the rooms she'd occupied had since that time remained unlet. Lu Xun records how, on a summer evening, driven out of doors by heat and the mosquitoes, he would sit beneath this tree, idly fanning himself and looking up into the chinks of sky just visible between its leaves, the late-emerging caterpillars dropping every so often, ice-cold, onto his neck.

This had been a lonely time, but life with the family too, it seems, did not go as expected, for in 1923, not long after Eroshenko's departure, deteriorating relations with the older of his brothers drove him from the Badaowan house. Taking his mother and Zhu An, he settled, finally, in the house at 21 Third Lane, Fuchengmennei. This house, filling the northwest corner of the museum complex, could be seen now to our left, its evidently preserved quality contrasting strangely with the bustle of the streets outside and with the style of the newer buildings, housing the museum and an exhibition hall, which lay before us.

The museum, as it turned out, had few visitors, so we could take our time, though with English nowhere in evidence, and our limited Chinese, there was only the thick travelling dictionary in minuscule print on which to fall back to make sense of many of the captions. The main wall of the first room had been hung with images, each drawn from Lu Xun's Shaoxing childhood, each, what's more, already familiar to us from his writings. A tracing of the wedding procession from *The Mouse Gets Married*, which he'd kept pasted above his bed. Illustrations from *The Book of Mountains and Seas*, a fanciful treatment of foreign lands featuring nine-headed snakes, three-legged birds, a one-footed cow, and, as we could see now for ourselves, in perfect detail, headless monsters who used their nipples as eyes. Several photographs as well, in black and white, devoid of human presence, taken as it were after the fact. An empty stone stage by the river on which local operas were performed. A single tree near dusk, half out of focus, said to be the sweet osmanthus in the family courtyard under which the young Lu Xun would sit listening intently to the stories told him by his grandmother. And, much larger than the rest, grown grainy from enlargement, the kitchen of the Shaoxing house, with its fish-and-crab tile backsplash, and a worn stone cauldron in the foreground. It was in this kitchen, as a twelve-year-old, that Lu Xun first met Zhang Yunshui, the prototype for the peasant boy Runtu in "My Old Home," though, according to the caption, despite their differences in class (unlike the narrator and adult Runtu of the story, between whom a thick wall has grown up), the two of them remained good friends throughout their lives.

Throughout the other rooms, many familiar elements were also to be found, scattered, as it were, at random, among the items on display. George Bernard Shaw, in several group photos, the unmistakable beard jutting out at an improbable angle. The floor plan of a building which turned out to be the Shaoxing Hostel, its scholar tree, seen from above, in outline, like a child's drawing of a cloud. Across from it, another photo, this one of a big-boned handsome man, leaning in close beside Lu Xun even as he towered over him, eyes closed, against an unnamed backdrop, that could only be his good friend Eroshenko — he of the artless fondness for ducklings, tadpoles, duck ponds, and all things agricultural, a fondness that seemed to tug at their expressions, a source of much mutual delight and mock admonishment, as they composed themselves for the camera. Here too what appeared to be the original anatomy notebook, hand-corrected in red pen, from Lu Xun's medical school days. And beside it, gazing steadily out from its frame, the face of Professor Fujino, whose red pen it was that had decorated these pages with such a painstaking kindness. This farewell portrait, presented to Lu Xun on the occasion of his abandoning the study of medicine — ostensibly for biology — must have cast a questioning silence from its place on the wall, as the former student, returned to China and now living in Beijing, bent instead on restoring the curative powers of literature, sat writing deep into the night.

Farther on, another carefully prepared schematic, on which various salient features had been numbered and detailed, covering what would have otherwise been the extensive grounds just to the west of it, accompanied a scale model of the Badaowan house: here was the room where Lu Xun wrote; the pond where Eroshenko raised his tadpoles; a patch of what, had it been numbered, would have been the grass pulled up with much commotion and devoured, in its entirety, by Eroshenko's ducklings. Farther still, still freshly ironed in its glass case, though now emptied of its occupant, lay a faded cotton "long gown," the likes of which appeared in many of the photographs that lined the various museum walls, the last of these showing a now much aged Lu Xun in a café in Shanghai, eleven days before his death, laughing and smoking with a group of younger artists and their writer friends, his generosity expressed, as ever, in his high hopes for the future.

A case near the stairs to the exit held the final exhibit, a plaster mask made on his deathbed — by a friend or neighbour — *which* was not made clear — only the man's name (Okuda), his profession (dentist) and his nationality (Japanese). This face, or rather mask of a face, appeared to be facing neither forwards nor backwards but rather nowhere at all, as though startled, momentarily, at being so newly absent from the world.

We'd spent several hours in what was, after all, not a large museum, and my friend, who'd stayed behind, undaunted by the unfamiliar characters, determined to decipher what he could, still hadn't caught up to me. Tracking back, I found him finally, studying a caption on the wall above a wooden desk into whose top surface a single character had been inexpertly carved. One day, according to the caption, Lu Xun, then still a schoolboy, having arrived late for his tutoring and received a scolding from his teacher, had taken it upon himself to carve this small *zao* — "early, in advance" — into his desktop, as a daily remonstrance and reminder. Such resolve, so obviously well-suited to a future literary conscience of the nation, no doubt has some truth to it, but at the same time, the precocious rectitude it conjures should be tempered by the stories of a much more impish Lu Xun — one constructing finger warriors in paper helmets who'd engage in heated battles while the teacher's back was turned.

Leaving the exhibition hall, crossing a small parking area, we came at last to Lu Xun's former residence. Built in the Beijing courtyard style, it was bought in 1924 and redesigned to Lu Xun's specifications. Troops of writers and artists almost immediately began to make their way along Third Lane, a flow that stopped only in 1926 when, having offended local warlords, he was forced to flee south, taking his lover, Xu Guangping, and leaving his mother and Zhu An behind. Over the next ten years he would return here only twice, while giving lectures in Beijing. During this period, his mother and Zhu An lived much as they had before, preserving the house and artifacts, first in his absence, then after his death as well. When after a further seven years his mother also died, Zhu An carried on this task alone.

Entering the courtyard, we found the house watched over by a single middle-aged woman in a small service vestibule who sat drinking tea and reading, looking up at us from time to time. Two leafy trees, planted originally with his own hands, and now propped up with wooden struts, cast their shadows down into the courtyard, just outside the study window. A visitor in 1936, come to make funeral arrangements in the first days following his death, found the Tiger's Tail — the study where he worked and took his meals, then slept after the last of the visitors who'd come to smoke and drink and argue late into the night had left — already turned into a kind of shrine. Peering with difficulty through the different panes, shielding our eyes against the surface glare, we could make out a reclining bed, some books, a writing desk. When after a while we'd not moved on, the woman turned her book, still open to the page that she'd been reading, face down on her chair, and came across to us. The conversation that ensued established that we'd come from Canada, knew of Bethune, lived in Toronto (which was not that far from Gravenhurst), and that the story of the doctor's sacrifice, told in Mao's famous essay, had moved her as a younger woman. Also that we'd read Lu Xun, as she suspected, and would like to see inside.

Taking a set of keys out from an inner pocket, she went round the courtyard opening the doors, then, leaving us to inspect things at our leisure, went back to her book again. An empty rattan chair sat squared against the writing desk, and on the desk, the lamp he'd used, a clock, some writing brushes upright in a bamboo rack, a teacup with its lid on, but no ink or paper. Across the way, the rooms where Zhu An and his mother lived what was essentially a separate life had also been (albeit sparsely) furnished, a few representative period pieces serving more as a reminder of their one-time occupation of these rooms than as a reconstruction of that life. Around a corner at the back, behind the Tiger's Tail, we came upon a neat bare yard with a disused well at its center, surrounded by a patch of desiccated grass. A few aging trees and a yellow thorn-plum bush still grew there, and along the crevice in a boundary wall, a nameless small-leafed vine was climbing. From the back wall of the Tiger's Tail, a bank of windows looked out on this scene.

In "My Old Home" Runtu arrives, to visit and "pay his respects," not long after the narrator's return. Although the two of them were once fast friends, it is thirty years since they last met. Runtu has brought with him his fifth son, Shuisheng, who is shy at first, so shy he hides behind his father and will not "bow to the Master." Only when Hong'er takes him out to play, much as the narrator and Runtu had as children, is he finally at ease. Famine and taxes, bandits, local gentry, the hard life of the peasant — all have taken their toll, and the mother of the narrator who, hearing voices, has come downstairs to smooth the awkwardness, suggests, when Runtu finally is out of earshot, that they offer him those things they won't be taking with them, allowing him to choose. That afternoon he chooses two long tables, a few chairs, some ceremonial items, and the ash heaps from the cooking fires to use as fertilizer, arranging to come back with a boat to pick them up the morning of the family's departure. When that day arrives, he's one among the many visitors who come and go, some to see the family off, some to pick up items, others to do both. As the day goes on, the house grows more and more depleted, till near evening everything is finally cleared away, and it is time to go.

From where we stood behind the Tiger's Tail, that sense of emptiedness now seemed to radiate in all directions, the yard where we were standing, the carefully preserved, half-furnished house calling to

mind not just that scene again but, simultaneously, the unlet rooms in the Shaoxing Hostel, and our teacher's childhood in the hills, with its no-longer-in-existence family home. Leaving the museum compound, which was now about to close, we stopped for dinner at a local restaurant, then made our way once more along Third Lane, the houses to either side, receding in our wake, seeming to turn a faint blue in the shadows of the not-quite-evening light.

It's June, and my visit to Lu Xun's house has already receded more than a year and many hundreds of kilometers into the past. This is the trouble with writing. As soon as something is written down it is no longer happening *now*, but can only have taken place "back then," "some time ago," finally "way back then," until at last it exists only as story, in the indeterminate once-upon-a-time.

Some time ago then, on an August trip to Beijing, in an era Lu Xun could not have imagined, we visited the Lu Xun Museum, in the Xicheng district, not far from Fuchengmen. What from the classroom in Toronto had seemed distant and exotic — Beijing, the Forbidden City, Lu Xun's residence, even the local accent, in which we could hear our teacher talking of her Xiangshan childhood — all were close at hand. Xiangshan and the Western Hills lay not far to the west of us, and on that same trip, a week or so later, we decided to make an excursion there.

We set out in the cool of the early morning, boarding first a crowded city bus, and then the subway. What with the fast pace of construction in the city, our guidebook's transit information (though no more than a year old) had proved often obsolete, and this turned out to be the case again, none of the bus stops for the routes to Xiangshan being in their promised places just outside the exit to the Pingguoyuan station, the last stop on the east-west subway line. After a half-hour in the growing heat, circling the nearby blocks without success, we decided to set out along the main road, in the direction of Xiangshan. Several of the Xiangshan buses passed us on our way, but, after a further half-hour's walk, we'd still not come to any of their stops. A number of rickety private minibuses, which also ran into the hills, had passed us by already, some without doors, others with seats, seen through an open door, held down with rope or duct tape. The next of these that came along, as had the others, slowed down to a walking pace beside us, the hoarse-voiced conductress, leaning precipitously from a side door, yelling out the various destinations, among which was Xiangshan. Boarding the still-just-moving bus, we found ourselves a broken seat and space on a wheel-well cover, and were finally on our way. The bus now continued in the general direction of the hills, slowing down as it neared each unmarked, but apparently official, stop, allowing riders to hop on or off, then speeding up, the dilapidated doors swinging half-shut as it did so, the conductress all the while continuing her monologue, collecting fares and making change, keeping a lookout for potential customers among those still out walking along the road.

To each side, acre after acre of what had recently been farmland had been parcelled up into housing and condominium developments, and many of the older houses that remained along the road were now in various stages of demolishment. As the land rose, the traffic swelled, the road clogged now not with the bicycles and old-fashioned farm vehicles of the China of ten years prior, but with taxis and brand-new private cars. Finally the two-lane road filled up completely, and our bus came to a halt. After some time standing there, not having moved an inch, our driver, evidently laconic by nature, with a nod to the conductress, simply swerved the bus up onto the uneven dirt shoulder, and we bumped our way past the double column of traffic, past the minor accident with its swarm of officials that had been the cause of our delay, and sailed on without further ado to the small market town at the base of Xiangshan.

The streets of the town were thronged with people, most part of the crowd that snaked its way uphill along the main route leading on into the park. A smattering of early risers, on their way back down already, moved against the flow. The street was narrow, more so for the shopfronts lining either side, before which all manner of goods had been laid out for sale. Gigantic baskets of cape gooseberries just now in season, pinwheels in the shapes of butterflies, gaudy plastic souvenirs in geometric arrays, and next to these, towers of bottled water sweating in the heat, laminated postcards bearing last year's maple leaves, bins of nuts and dried fruits overseen by wasps. Now and then a car approached, nudging its way ahead into the crowd, the festive atmosphere, divided in its presence, re-forming seamlessly behind it. The journey to this point had been not only more eventful, but much longer than intended, leaving us both hot and thirsty, and already hungry in the bargain. As luck would have it, just outside the east gate, near the ticket counters, was a map showing the main features of the park, among these several snack bars and a large hotel, the Xiangshan, just inside the park boundary. A tree-lined road led off in that direction.

Built with a certain fanfare in the early eighties, and subsequently made even more famous by the rising fame of its architect, I. M. Pei, the Xiangshan turned out to be, if no longer the pinnacle of luxury it must once have seemed, nonetheless extremely pleasant. Around a large open foyer with a fountain which, at intervals, sprang unexpectedly to life, its sound mimicking a bubbling spring, or brook, were four separate restaurants, each with its own regional cuisine. We hadn't been seated long, ordering the local beer and two dishes in the Sichuan restaurant, when we looked up to find a tall, stately woman, wearing a large, black, floppy hat and oversized rhinestone-studded sunglasses, apparently making straight for our table.

It's not uncommon, in China, for foreigners to find themselves approached by those who are able to speak some English and hence eager to communicate while, at the same time, practicing the language with a native speaker. Exchanging a glance, we prepared ourselves for the usual conversation: where we were from, whether we'd been to China previously, had we seen places other than Beijing, how many children did we have, how long would we be staying...?

But now, without a word, having arrived at our table, the woman removed her hat and sunglasses. It was none other than our old teacher, Shu-Ying.

Over all the years that both we and Shu-Ying have lived in Toronto, we've never once run into one another on the street, yet now, through a series of accidents of mutual timing, here she was, standing beside our table halfway around the world. She was here, she told us, on an impulse, having decided to fly over the week before classes started to visit her son, a Hong Kong movie actor who happened to be involved in a joint production, shooting on location in Beijing. Even so, she added — the mother in her coming out — she'd barely seen him. Each night since she'd arrived he'd come home late after the shoot, when she'd already fallen asleep. The son, the rather craggily handsome man now looking on in a slightly sheepish manner from a table at the far end of the room, had clearly had no choice in the matter — he'd taken the day off to accompany his mother on a visit to the site of her old family home.

The house where her family had lived, she continued, along with several other houses and the school, had been demolished, the land re-appropriated by the government to make way for the hotel. Our chance meeting (it now dawned on us) was thus taking place, not just near, but on the exact site of, our teacher's childhood home. Much of what would have defined that childhood time was therefore gone, fully expunged — yet much else was now part of the official history, and hence more fully preserved than it would otherwise have been. Nearby was Spectacles Lake, where she'd learned to skate; the path through the pines toward the faded red-walled ruins of Xiangshan Temple; hillsides of smoke trees which in autumn blazed with colour, each branch within easy reach stripped bare by those come from the city to enjoy the spectacle. But her favourite spot in all of Xiangshan, the one we must make certain not to miss, was Shuangqing Villa. As a girl she'd gone there often, after school was out, walking there and back, alone through the forest.

The Western Hills, of which Xiangshan forms a part, are laid out (as one municipal brochure puts it) in the shape of a dustpan, from which, on a clear day, one can look out over the entire Beijing Plain. The site of a temple in ancient days, of an imperial hunting ground and park reserved for the emperor and palace retinue through the Ming and Qing, Xiangshan remains even now a favourite place to escape the summer heat. And so at Spectacles Lake, at the height of summer, having finished our lunch and said goodbye to Shu-Ying and her son, we stood gazing out over the water, imagining our teacher as a young girl still in braids gliding easily across its surface. Then, following the paths that criss-crossed up into the hills, we made our way to Shuangqing Villa.

The villa — Shuangqing: double springs, clear double fountain — sits on the site of an old imperial garden. The name dates to the 1920s, when the garden was converted into a luxurious private residence and the phrase, ostensibly in the Emperor Qianlong's handwriting, was carved into the lintel of a peaked stone gateway through which the visitor is meant to enter. From this vantage point, a small rectangular water-lily pool, fed by two underground springs and overhung by pines and gingkos, could be seen, the tranquility of the scene no less effective for having been so carefully constructed. Extending from a platform jutting out into the water on the far side, the inverted image of a red hexagonal pavilion intermingled with the half-opened lilies, and though it was only August, a few gingko leaves, turned prematurely yellow and fallen to the pool, now and then began to twist erratically, as if suspended just above the surface.

In the background lay the villa proper, a low, one-storey building with a stone base and a grey-tiled, gabled roof. Shadows played across the whitewashed walls and, now and then, a group of passersby would stop to point out something written on a sign, then peer in through the open door, or press their faces to the red-framed windows. Following their lead, we learned what every schoolchild brought here from the city would have known already, namely that in March of 1949, Mao Zedong, together with the other members of the Central Committee of the soon-to-be-victorious CCP, came here from the countryside to set up headquarters. It was thus in this very building that the "Campaign to Cross the Yangtze" was planned, in these grounds that the blueprints for a new China, one that seemed now within easy reach, were drawn up. People alive at the time, even those soon to be caught up in the Anti-Rightist purges of the 1950s, talk of the sense of optimism in the air. A representative official history has been preserved here. Faded war maps still pinned to the walls. Mao's bed, neatly made. Some papers, ashtrays, a few books, the desk with its telephone straight out of a 1940s movie, overstuffed armchairs once meant for visitors, their leather stiff with age. That new life, if it ever existed, has long since passed these by.

❖

Not long ago, returning from another visit to Beijing, I stopped in at one of the many duty-free shops at the Beijing Capital airport. Among the usual perfumes and souvenirs and cigarettes, the vast array of alcohols over which my eye had been passing in an effort to kill some time before the flight, was a display of tall blue cardboard boxes, of the sort in which special liquors, intended to be bought as gifts, are often sold. On the front of these boxes, which closer inspection revealed to be constructed of a rather beautiful, apparently handmade, paper, embossed in gold, were the characters of Lu Xun's name, part of the phrase "In Memoriam, Lu Xun." A cut had been made into the surface of each box, forming a triangular wedge that could be flipped back to reveal a dark blue velvet lining and the ceramic bottle, presumably of Shaoxing wine, contained within, the top part of which consisted of a bust of Lu Xun. This bust, which closely resembled that standing just inside the entrance to the Lu Xun Museum complex, stared straight ahead, unmoved, and remembering that earlier visit, I had no choice but to buy it as a gift for my companion from that trip, who would soon be waking for the morning in Toronto, anticipating my return.

Near the end of "My Old Home," some time after boarding the boat that is to take them away forever from their old hometown, the narrator is finally left alone on deck. Before falling asleep, his nephew Hong'er has been talking with him, somewhat mournfully, but also with excitement, once more mentioning his new friend Shuisheng and asking when they will be coming back. Watching the familiar landscape slip away and turning this over, hearing the steady sound of waves beneath the boat, it occurs to him that, though he and Runtu have been cut off from one another, the generation to follow still has much in common — that another life may yet be possible, a new life, one they themselves have never experienced. He then goes on to say: "This arrival of hope made me suddenly fearful. When Runtu had asked for the candlesticks and incense burner, I'd secretly laughed at him, thinking that he was still worshiping idols, and would never be free of them. But wasn't what I was now calling hope not also an idol, though one I had constructed myself? The only difference was what he desired was near at hand, while what I desired was vastly more distant."

Toward the end of his life, Lu Xun's sympathies veered more and more toward the Left. But though sympathetic to their aims, and despite much pressure to do otherwise, he never joined the CCP. In a famous 1927 lecture, "The Divergent Paths of Art and Politics," he expressed the opinion that politics and literature, by the nature of the latter, would always be in opposition. Asked what Lu Xun would have had to do, had he still been alive in the 1950s, Mao is said to have remarked, "'Conform to the trend,' or go to jail." This despite the near deification of Lu Xun and his works, the image of the revolutionary writer as exemplar, promulgated on the mainland in the period since 1949.

"When I was young I too," writes Lu Xun, "had many dreams, most of which I subsequently forgot, though this does not seem to me a cause for regret. Such memories, though they can often bring happiness, at other times cannot help but bring loneliness as well . . . and what is the point of that? My problem is that I am unable to forget completely, and it is out of those things I have been unable to forget completely up till now that *A Call to Arms* has been made."

Reading this now from the comfort of my own home in Toronto, which has always seemed to me in some way "temporary," I watch the stormclouds rolling in, bringing with them the rumble of June thunder. In Beijing, no doubt, as here, the sidewalks will be black with fallen mulberries, the branches loud with the rasping of cicadas. From this distance, I begin to wonder: could it really have been Lu Xun who carved that small *zao* into the desk? Would such a desk have survived outside of the story about it? And what of the anatomy notebook? Didn't Lu Xun himself, in his memoir of Professor Fujino, say the notebooks had been lost? The desk, I find myself thinking, is a replica, the *zao* a well-intentioned fake, meant to arouse the visitor's heart. And what if the real notebooks were indeed all lost, or the desk re-made — what exactly would have been preserved, and what betrayed, by such small alterations in what, in all probability, is an already altered version of the facts?

In the famous ending to "My Old Home" — which the polemical surround of the decades since his death apparently makes unreadable to some — the narrator, himself now also drifting toward sleep, finds suddenly before him a scene echoing his childhood days with Runtu. "Before my eyes," he begins, "a broad expanse of jade-green seashore had been spread, above which, in the deep blue sky, hung a round yellow moon. I thought: hope can neither be said to exist, nor said not to exist. In this it is just like the roads of the earth. For actually, to begin with the earth has no roads, but where many people pass, there a road is made."

Formed with even fewer strokes than the little *zao* once inscribed in a desktop by a young Lu Xun is the word *wen*, which means pattern, writing, literature. Along with *person*, *mouth*, and *mother*, it is among the first words taught to foreigners. Such patterns, *wen*, are considered to constitute a natural property, or rather configuration, of the world: in the enigmatic flow of events as in the shapes of the written language; in the shapes of the written language as in the mind of literature; in the mind of literature as in the cosmos.

I myself have travelled along paths laid down by others who have gone before me. Such paths, like Lu Xun's narrator's hope, can neither be said to exist nor not to exist. Nonetheless, the figure of Lu Xun remains nearby, a now-near-empty bottle of Shaoxing wine left standing on a bookshelf in Toronto where it keeps giving off sparks, hints and glimpses of a hot

Beijing morning, echoes of our teacher's childhood home, incidents receding years and kilometers into the past, where stories are formed.

Lu Xun died in 1936, and therefore I can never meet him in this life, or presume to guess his feelings. Even so, a certain title, "Lu Xun's Desk," keeps intruding into my waking thoughts, reasserting itself again and again, keeping up an unreasonable pressure, at last urging me to write it down — as though merely by writing something down, something more might be accomplished.

We were some way already into our conference excursion, wending our way behind our Chinese guides and stopping dutifully before each point of interest, when the old scholar turned and, looking me straight in the eyes, said, "□□□, □□□□□□, □□□□," and then repeated it for emphasis.

We had come, fifteen or so of us in all, and in the presence of three of the conference organizers, well-known Chinese physicists whose sense of hospitality dictated a day of shepherding us about, managing meals and transportation, acting as guides and, most important, serving as interpreters, to the shores of the miniature panoramic lake in the midst of the Grandview Garden, near the town of Zhouzhuang, on the outskirts of Shanghai. The garden is a replica — one of only two in existence at the time — of the garden of the same name in the famous eighteenth-century novel *Honglou Meng* (The Dream of the Red Mansions) by Cao Xueqin, which the old scholar could undoubtedly recite by heart.

A short cruise on the nearby lake had been arranged for our arrival, followed by a formal welcome in which, in an honour usually reserved for VIPs, the garden's senior scholar was to be presented to us, and then take us on our tour. The Scholar of the Garden, as it turned out, was a man into his seventies who, having lived through the political upheavals of the decades previous, wore a simple cotton suit and cloth shoes, in a style common to that era. White-bearded and leaning heavily on his walking stick, he looked to be very frail indeed, yet could speak at impressive length on any aspect of the garden — those scenes that had taken place there, and their role in the novel's larger structure. Informed that there were two among this group of foreigners who'd read the novel (albeit only in translation), he went on with considerable animation, leaving little room for interruption (even for translation!).

"□□□, □□□□, □□, □□□□□□, □□□, □□□□," he continued, his attention now squarely on me as he spoke, with an occasional nod of recognition and/or confirmation to my companion, and under this influence, and without any knowledge of the language, I *did* begin (whether from a sense of duty, or responsibility, or simply wishing that it might be so) to feel that I could understand. The other foreign visitors who, like us, could not speak the language, had begun to shift uncomfortably, unfamiliar with the story and so interested only in the garden's pure *Chineseness* — yet the Scholar of the Garden (a title reflecting not only his current position, but also his manifest qualifications for the job), unmoved by their restiveness, pressed on, and in an ever more determined, almost reckless, manner.

For some time we'd been shadowed by a group of locals, who'd watched us, in our role of "honoured guests," being taken behind cordons, backstage as it were, into the numerous pavilions where, for instance, props and costumes for the re-enactments of the novel's key scenes might be stored, or into rooms containing reproductions of the porcelains and paintings belonging to the family in the novel — areas off-limits to the normal visitor. Now and then there had been catcalls, evidently aimed at us. Eventually one of the organizers had taken up our cause, the interchanges (said to be "too difficult to translate") escalating until, finally, kicks and punches were exchanged, and both groups, in the interest of public order, had to drag their champions apart.

"Drunk," the organizer commented dismissively, somewhat calmer now — and indeed the other man's face was a dark dusky red, though whether with drink or fury would have been hard to say. Both had taken blows to the face, and the organizer, a square-shaped, hearty fellow from Sichuan, whose candour — one year to the day after the "incident" at Tiananmen, and in a far from private setting — had already surprised us earlier that week, now sported a black eye, which darkened perceptibly with the passing hours, lending him the air of an adventuresome bandit or dashing rake.

Among those who turn up their noses at the likes of the West Edmonton Mall, Colonial Williamsburg, or Paris Disneyland, most, no doubt, would view the Grandview Garden with a similar mistrust, avoiding it, therefore, with an equally avid disdain. It may be worth considering, though, that the novel on which the garden is based, itself once deemed vulgar, now holds a long-standing reputation for drawing scholars and readers alike into its world, sometimes to a degree that friends and family find uncomfortable. The book's most respected English translator, for one, convinced that he might never regain a foothold in his own proper life, famously handed over the project to a son-in-law, having reached precisely that point in the novel where the original author had exited this world, leaving his great unfinished work behind — in effect, to the uncertain ministrations of a follower (whether a cousin, nephew, or posthumous friend) who then had to cobble together the entire last third of the novel from the dead man's notes. There has been much discussion over the years as to whether the ending as it stands represents the original author's intentions, or whether the plot was in fact interfered with by an inferior imagination, even deliberately adulterated perhaps, a charge of some seriousness, especially with regard to a book of such delicate balances. The details of the debate blur, yet the book remains: a beautiful, sprawling, two-thousand-page dalliance of indecision between two extremes of beauty.

In our travels so far we've come across three separate cities in southern China (any one of which might once have boasted mansion gardens of comparable layout and size) each offering itself up as the original source for the novel's setting and inspiration. Prince Gong's Garden in Beijing also has its advocates, and indeed the author is known to have spent the last six years of his life working on his novel while living in considerable poverty in the Western Hills, on the outskirts of the city. Suffice it to say that there remain issues unlikely to be resolved by any amount of scholarship. In just such a way the book itself, like the garden in which we find ourselves standing, can be considered a replica of sorts, masterful yet crude, of the author's passing thoughts and experiences. All large novels have their devotees, but there is a particular pathos attached to the unfinished masterpiece which seems to draw scholars into it as into an abyss. Robert Musil's *The Man Without Qualities* comes to mind (another massive, involuntarily abandoned work), though no one to my knowledge has offered to take up the novel at the point where Musil was forced to leave off. On the other hand, it may be that all of literature, seen from a certain vantage point and as a whole, has this unfinished quality, which draws us into it as into life itself.

In the two decades since I first visited Shanghai, the city has undergone numerous unwieldy changes. And though I've often thought of revisiting the Grandview Garden, especially now that I have a few words of the language, enough to be able to make my own way there on the local bus, I feel I'd rather not disturb my old memories, or have to see them replaced. That such a man should have become engaged with such intensity, and over matters of such obvious importance, with so unlikely a person seems implausible — and did so even then. Nonetheless, by the time we reached the moon window which looks out on the small private garden of Lin Daiyu, the frail and sickly beauty of the novel, I felt I understood what he intended, almost as an old friend might. "Sit here," he indicated, pointing to the concrete sill of the moon window, and, just as distinctly, "Take her picture now," to my companion. Perhaps, you think, this is a kind of set piece, yet another standard feature of a standard tour: to pose the youngest woman of the group as Lin Daiyu. But to what point, I wonder, when the group consists of foreigners?

Studying this photograph, I find myself astonished by that now much younger self. I wish the old scholar were also in the photograph, but he is not. The date, recorded on the back, is *June 6, 1990. Grandview Garden, Near Shanghai*, it says. We've set out at eleven, and have stopped for lunch along the way, so it is nearly two when we arrive. At the restaurant, many local specialties have been prepared, a stewed eel in particular, which the foreign guests have picked at stiffly while a group of cadres looks on in amusement from a private room. Earlier a light rain has been falling, but the skies have cleared. Our bus has left the conference venue, edging out onto the main street, joining what few vehicles there are amidst a sea of bicycles. Public buses, army transports, trucks with goods of various descriptions — lurch past in a state of constant near-collision, creeping in and out of momentary gaps, horns blaring. Along the roadsides we can see (more so of course in retrospect) the stirrings of a new commercial China: a man with three small oranges on a scrap of newsprint, someone nearby with what looks like four zucchinis, one of which has just been sold, another with six packs of cigarettes (American, it seems) stacked in a perfect ziggurat, and so on. They squat calmly, with their arms about their knees, and chat to passersby, rising to leave when what they've brought is sold. After lunch, we leave the city proper. In the fields, grand new houses built by farmers suddenly made wealthy by the produce from their private plots appear. Soon we will reach the garden, and there be presented to the Scholar, who as yet does not exist for us.

Commenting on the art of portraiture in his eighteenth-century treatise on painting, Shen Zongqian observes:

> The reason the ancients don't talk of transmitting the outward shape or appearance, but only of transmitting the spirit, is that there are in the world examples of people having the same outward shape or similar appearance, though it is of course impossible for the spirits to be the same. If the painter concentrates only on outward likenesses, then among sufficiently many others will be those who also resemble the portrait, and how could this be considered a true likeness? Now before you is a person. Where once he was fat, now he is thin; where once he was youthful, now he has greyed; where once he was clean-shaven, now he has a full beard. Yet when you see him, you think to yourself that this is so-and-so — perhaps much changed, but nonetheless, still so-and-so. This is because outward form changes, but the spirit does not. If in a painting there is a small loss of likeness in the outward form, that is still alright, but the slightest variation in the spirit, and the man you wished to paint is lost.

As for the author Cao Xueqin, there is a single portrait of him, by a well-known artist of the time, believed by some to show him in the year before his death. The subject is a short, good-humoured man, with a drinker's countenance, and matches well enough descriptions of him found elsewhere. A truer portrait, though, is to be found among the poems and letters of his friends, who knew about the book, and in the decade leading up to his death urged him, repeatedly, to get on with the work of bringing it to some conclusion, keeping him in wine so he would not have to subject himself to the constraints that come of "knocking on the doors of rich men's houses." Evidently familiar with its contents, they refer frequently to his "dream of the South," or "dream of departed/vanished splendours." In the thirty years following his death, the novel went unpublished, but was circulated privately, and widely spoken of. In the public sphere, a literary inquisition raged, and many writers subsequently lost their lives over perceived slights to the Qianlong emperor. It was during this time that key portions of the author's drafts, now known to have existed, and covering, at least in part, the last third of the novel, were misplaced, or lost, or (much more likely in the climate of the times) actively suppressed by members of the family. The stature of the novel — and this sense, in consequence, of its political significance — is a constant of the series of upheavals that make up the history of post-dynastic China. The battles of the "new Red-ologists" against the "old Red-ologists." The modernist/conservative and leftist/pragmatist debates that mark the decade following the May

Fourth Movement. Mao Zedong's mass movement against expert — but politically suspect — opinion, launched, in 1954, with the attack on then-existing critical assessments of the *Honglou Meng*. In 1966, the book was, for a time, itself proscribed — part of a ban incorporating all pre-revolutionary literature and Western works, the nineteenth-century Russian tracts on which the social-realist approach was based among them. Asking a friend for details of this ban, we found ourselves, having been passed from one acquaintance to the next, on to the next, and so on, rapidly across the room and through the middle of the party going on around us, finally presented to an older woman, who'd been twenty at the time and living in Beijing. She recalled that, though decisions of this type were usually preceded by much acrimonious public "debate," no official statement of this ban was ever made — the book simply became "unavailable," except by unofficial means, meaning it might be picked up after closing at the back door of the library, read furiously with friends over the next week, and then returned as it had come, leaving the nominal status quo intact. At some point, once more without public notice, it became "available" again. A publisher's note to the 1978 Beijing Foreign Languages Press edition, translated by Gladys Yang and Yang Hsien-yi — a note which would have been composed not long after the death of Mao, and still, to a large extent, in the long shadows cast by the final throes of the Great Cultural Revolution — records the tenor of the times, and reads in part:

A Dream of Red Mansions is a book about political struggle, a political-historical novel. . . . Regarding the novel's objective artistic effect, it undoubtedly exposes and attacks the feudal system from various angles; hence its main ideological tendency is good. This does not mean, however, that the work contains no feudal dross and the author's world outlook no feudal ideas. For after all, Cao Xueqin was born into a declining noble family more than two hundred years ago. . . . His pessimism and fatalistic, nihilistic ideas, his view of life as a tragedy and all on earth as vanity, as well as his feudal approach to certain matters show the clear brandmark of the author's class origin and times. . . .

These are the waters a man like the Scholar would have had to navigate — in what ways it is impossible for us to know.

Sometimes now when I sit down to dip into the novel — reminding myself, in a moment of leisurely boredom, of this or that particular scene — I find him once more at my side, pointing out a certain writing brush, a storeroom made for storing kites, another play on words I've failed to notice until now. Writes Hayden White: "While annals represent historical reality as if real events did not display the form of a story, the chronicle represents it as if real events appeared to human consciousness in the form of *unfinished* stories." Seen in the light of a history of narrative, our encounter in the Grandview Garden may appear less enigmatic, less of an isolated event. One of the many populating some much larger work, which, like the novel, will at some point end, though it cannot be said to have "been finished."

One summer day some years ago, travelling in a far province, I managed to catch up with an old friend. This was shortly after I'd returned from China and the Grandview Garden, and, as my time was short, our meeting had involved much juggling of mutual schedules. We were lounging on a grassy hill, finishing our picnic and talking of many things, when suddenly she began to relate an experience she'd had as a child. Her parents, who were going out for the evening, had left her for a few hours in the care of a favourite uncle. She'd been tucked into bed only to waken a short time later, perplexed by a strange sound. Tiptoeing out along the darkened hall, she peered around a corner into the living room, from which, it seemed, the sound was emanating. There she saw her uncle, sitting on a couch in the light of a lamp, reading aloud. The eerie, amazing sound — unlike anything she'd ever heard before — was coming from him. The book from which he'd been reading was a very early collection of Chinese poetry, rendered aloud in the peculiar chanting rhythms of the original. That uncle — her much-loved Uncle David — would have been no more than a young man at the time, still a student in fact. Over the course of his life, he was to become one of the most famous translators of the twentieth century. Many years of that illustrious career were spent immersed in the work of translating the first two-thirds of Cao Xueqin's novel, the last third (as we know already) having later been handed on to a much younger man. These three, Wendy Martin, David Hawkes, John Minford the son-in-law, thus join the Scholar of the Garden in our still-unfinished story.

"Who are these characters," asks the author's brother, in his introduction to the first chapter of the novel, "and what was the author's purpose in writing this book?" He answers with his brother's own words: "Having made an utter failure of my life, I found myself one day, in the midst of my poverty and wretchedness, thinking about the companions of my youth. . . . As I recalled them, one by one, I found myself being overwhelmed by regrets, and resolved, then and there, to make a record of those days."

It is twenty years since I first set eyes on the piece of
land that was to become a home in my mind. It came
at the end of an afternoon of being shown a number
of properties in the vicinity, none of which matched
our expectations. As soon as we walked up the gravel
drive and looked out on the view now spread below,
we turned our heads and simply nodded to each
other. It is still the only spur-of-the-moment pur-
chase we have ever made. In that place, each leaf and
flower, each trunk and rocky outcrop, has not only
its own vibrant life, but states itself, or stands forth,
as a clear recollection of a prior order. It is for this
reason that I can live there in my mind, while at the
same time spending my actual days in another place,
a place that has a continuous chaotic life about it but
no former existence. Poetry does not allow one to
live where one would wish, but only where one can.
It is a stepping-stone existence.

When the property passed from the previous
owners' hands and into ours, the land was every-
where festooned with pampas grass and stonecrop.
The driveway (which turned out to be a former
logging road) was steep and gravelled. Much has
changed since then. The land has been reasserting
itself in our absence, and is subject to no human law.
In that time, we have seen, first, small trees begin to
fill the drive, then broom, whose branches, lit with
yellow blossoms, point the way from spring through

fall. Larger trees have grown up too, and some have even fallen with the winter storms. It is all we can do, on our infrequent visits, to keep a narrow path open, wide enough to pass in single file.

Over the years we have explored more and more of the full breadth and depth of the property, which is large, with most of its formal boundaries unmarked. Seen from above (which is to say as in the calculus of deeds and titles), it covers fourteen acres, but on foot the variations of the steep terrain, the knolls and upland meadows, sudden creek beds and, along one boundary line, set at the bottom of a permanently darkened hollow too precipitous to navigate, one deep round spring-fed pool, make it, in truth, much larger, less amenable to being contemplated outside its particulars. Here sunlight pools on a mossy rock, there a fallen tree serves as a bench from which to look out on the nearby standing trunks; here bark has been worn away where a buck has dispensed with a full year's growth of antlers, there a shadow falls across a patch of orange-green lichen. The world is stilled, growing at a slower pace, which ticks by soundlessly, measured by the creak of the arbutus, or a hawk's or eagle's crossing of that patch of sky visible beyond the crowns of fir and cedar.

One summer, for a full week, we hacked away at the broom that had overgrown what, in succession, had been first a driveway, then a path, and finally become impassable. We hung an old box kite, still brightly coloured but long past its flying days, in the branches of a broad-leafed maple anchored near the runoff ditch. After the big storm one year, we sawed the fallen trees that lay across the path and rolled the sections off to one side. Each time, shortly after finishing our labours, we would leave, and all that we'd accomplished would once more begin to be undone, the cycle of clearing and undoing, clearing and undoing, slowly, over the years, itself becoming part of the nature of that place.

These, of course, are just the ordinary experiences of living. We have never lived on that land, but visit it in reality as one might a place known only in imagination, keeping it as a talisman of some other, parallel, existence — a place where sunlight falls aslant through the woods, as if in a direct line from heaven.

Meanwhile, we occupy ourselves with tasks, living a modest life (though one which passes quickly) in a modest, rather ordinary, house a half a continent away, in that familiar, if chaotic, destination called the city. Many friends have come and gone during our time here. Some still live nearby, while others have moved to distant cities and are now seen only on occasion, passing through. A large, beautiful sumac used to grow wild in the southeast corner of our small backyard, and so the house was christened Sumac Cottage in its honour. That sumac has passed on, but a new one is growing close to where it spent its days, so Sumac Cottage is still an acceptable name, I would guess.

Who is it that owns these properties?

In spirit, if not in title: Baziju.

And what is the meaning of this name? Its derivation?

I can only answer: as in all acts of transformation, where two can become one, or one many, Baziju is a vessel for shared experience.

In 2002, during a trip to Shanghai, and after a long-ish conversation with my aunt in California who, though almost ninety, still remembered (vividly, it seemed) the little she'd been told about her mother's China days, we decided to go looking for one of the *shikumen* complexes still remaining in the city. Since our last visit, twelve years previous, a decade of explosive redevelopment had taken place, and I was hoping to track down some physical connection to my grandmother, who died before my birth, and who had spent the two years prior to her marriage living in Shanghai.

Growing up, my aunt and mother were sur-rounded by the clothes and jades and porcelains, the furniture their mother had brought back from China, but seldom heard her speak about her time there, and never thought to ask. Much that my aunt had had to pass on had been fleshed out or confirmed after her mother's death by Aunt Jo, a close friend of the family who had known her mother in Shanghai.

When they were girls, it was understood, by my aunt and mother at least — though never confirmed by either of the principals involved — that W. W. Taylor, the man the two of them called Uncle Double-Double, and whose visits, in my aunt's words, figured in their Berkeley childhoods, had once been engaged to my grandmother, when both were living in Shang-hai. By this time, my grandmother had been taken up by the American and British sets, and was teaching at St. Mary's Hall, hence reasonably well-off, but before that she'd spent a difficult half year living in a small room on the third floor of what, from my aunt's description, must have been a cut-up shikumen, a mode of cheap accommodation common in the city at that time. In this space, which she'd rented from an impoverished "second landlord" couple — an English clerk and his Eurasian wife who'd come from Hong Kong with the firm Jardine's, then fallen on hard times — she'd been eking out a living giving singing lessons to private pupils when she was "discovered," and rescued by Aunt Jo.

❖

My grandmother set off for China with little more than a sense of adventure, the promise of a job, and a quantity of Mexican silver dollars sewn into the hem of her skirt. This was in 1907. She'd just finished her sophomore year in college, but had too many debts to continue, and through missionary connections had been offered a job teaching singing in a small private girls' school in Shanghai. Not long after she decided to accept this offer, and not long before leaving for Shanghai, on a picnic in the Berkeley hills, arranged to take place at a spot they'd often gone before, with its sweeping view out over the Bay, to where the Golden Gate Bridge would one day be built, and beyond that, the Pacific, Ward Esterly — the man whom she'd been seeing for some time, and who was later to become my grandfather — asked her to marry him. She replied that she was going to China for a year, and would answer him on her return.

The trip from San Francisco to Shanghai took six weeks. In those days, most of the passengers would have been Americans who had just finished periods of home leave, and were now returning (usually with limited enthusiasm) to complete "the making of their fortunes" — after which they hoped to leave for good, and never have to see the place again. Such voyages (which the ships' crews called "returning the empties") were thus much less rambunctious affairs than the corresponding Shanghai–San Francisco trips.

Owing to the great quantities of silt carried by the Yangtze, and deposited at its mouth, only ships with the shallowest draughts were able to cross the bar at low tide. On arrival, therefore, most passenger liners had to wait some hours for high tide before crossing and making their way the remaining fourteen miles up the Yangtze, into the Huangpu, and thence, finally, on into Shanghai. A few miles of muddy foreshore, the jumbled roofs of Hongkou, beyond these Suzhou Creek, and then, at last, the sight of the opium hulks moored along the Bund, brought the passenger docks of the International Settlement, and the end of the voyage, into view.

It had been arranged that my grandmother would be met on the docks by a representative of the school, who would help with the luggage, and take her to the school's residence. Instead, she was met by a telegram saying that the school had folded, and there would be no job after all. By this point she'd been standing for some time, her luggage stacked around her, with a growing sense of trepidation. Periodically scanning the dock, she'd noticed a young man in Western clothing and a queue circulating through the crowd, carrying a square of stiff white paper which he was holding up to one female passenger after the other. When he came to her she saw the paper held a brief note, one written in a well-trained hand, which read

United States
San Francisco
Miss V. Judy

meaning the person he'd been looking for was her. Having ascertained, mostly by mutual noddings of the head, that she was, indeed, the said V. Judy, he handed her the telegram, bowed once, and left. The telegram said nothing about those who'd run the school, or what she was to do, and the money she had with her was nowhere near the cost of the return passage, so she was truly stuck. One of the pursers from the ship, who lived for part of each year in Shanghai, helped find her cheap accommodation, taking her there himself, her first experience of the city thus being the kaleidoscopic flash of half-scenes glimpsed in passing from the sprung seat of a pheasant rickshaw, a coolie with the steamer trunk and bags strung from a shoulder pole following at a trot close behind. Over the next few months she struggled, managed to find a few private students, and was eventually able to scrape together a living teaching Western music to the children of well-off Chinese. But this provided at best a subsistence existence, with no possibility of saving enough to pay her passage back.

Life among the shikumens must have come as something of a surprise to a young woman like my grandmother, who was the daughter of a Methodist minister, and had been brought up in modest, but comfortable, circumstances on the west coast of America. The belled carts and calls of the night-soil men waking the residents just before dawn, the clatter of clamshells as the nightstools were washed and the streets came slowly to life, the yells of the itinerant peddlers and street vendors who made their way into the alleyway compounds, setting up their stoves and stalls, selling all manner of food and goods, till late into the night. Certainly her time there is elided in the brief biographical note contained in the 1928 University of Oregon yearbook. That note, which accompanies a photograph of a very proper Mrs. V. Esterly, Dean of Women, has her attending the University of California at Berkeley and "going from there to St. Mary's School in Shanghai, where she served as Acting Head of the Department of Music from 1907–1910" — as if her time among the shikumens had never happened.

❖

In the early 1990s, the Chinese postal service issued a series of stamps depicting the *minju*, or ordinary people's dwellings, of various cities and regions in the country. A shikumen was chosen to represent Shanghai. In the decade immediately following, most of the city's shikumens were torn down and replaced with modern apartment towers. Knowing this, and hence that much of the old city would have been demolished, we'd come with articles, all published in the last few years, identifying neighbourhoods, and streets in each, in which the old-style shikumens could still be found.

The search at first seemed doomed. The two locations nearest our hotel had been completely re-developed: twelve- to twenty-storey blocks, already fully occupied, lined both sides of the streets. A third, farther location now lay stranded partway down the path toward the same end: trucks and labourers swarmed everywhere across the site, loading up the last of the debris from recent demolition work. Somewhat discouraged, we decided to try next an area near the main commercial district, mentioned in the most recent of the articles we'd brought. Our reasoning (more wishful, probably, than realistic by this point) was that, in its proximity to such tourist attractions as the Bund and Yu Yuan (a famous classical garden), and having been so recently described, this site might be more likely than the others to have dodged the wrecker's ball.

The neighbourhood around the Yu Yuan is a maze of narrow streets and market stalls. Most of the streets are unmarked, so it took us some time, not to mention several speculative realignments of the map, to reach our goal. When we did, we found only construction workers on their breaks and several half-completed apartment towers shrouded in bamboo scaffolding. A little weary from the day's exertions, and it being close at hand, we decided to take in the Yu Yuan, returning (this time more directly) as we'd come.

The entrance to the garden lies across a nine-bend zigzag bridge, which traverses a small lake, in the middle of which, accessible only via the bridge, is the Huxin Ting, a red two-storey teahouse built on stilts over the water. After the longish walk, the thought of sitting with a pot of green tea and a view over the lake and garden seemed unusually inviting, so we made our way up to the second floor. There we were seated at a window table in one of the large octagonal bays, looking out onto two of the garden's features, the Hall for Possessing the Moon and the Depository for Books and Paintings. An interior partition wall was hung with photographs — Deng Xiaoping and Jiang Zemin; the Clintons; Bruce Lee, Jackie Chan; various other grand, if somewhat lesser, dignitaries. Windows on the other walls held different garden views, one of the Toasting Hall, another of the Three Grain Ears Pavilion. An hour's idling over tea, and then a stroll around the garden, proved an excellent restorative, leaving us inclined to try the last site on our list.

This site, in the Jing'an Temple neighbourhood, had earlier seemed too unpromising to bother with, the article that mentioned it being focused on the plight of older areas of the city, already, at the time of writing, slated for near-term redevelopment. Now, simply by switching to a longer loop route back to our hotel, it could be seen as being "on our way." Entering the neighbourhood behind the temple, we soon found the area in question, as it turned out totally untouched. A short lane, lined with houses, led off from the main road. Near the entrance to the lane, a small dog on a leash bounded happily in circles round an older grey-haired woman standing near the entrance to her house, caught up in conversation with a similarly aged woman who'd just come out from the house next door. The two of them glanced now and then in our direction and then back to one another. Hoping they might know something of the compound's history, we went over to the lane, and waited. The dog immediately broke off its bounding, turning its attention to our shoes and cuffs, but neither of the women joined in in acknowledging our presence, and our attempts at conversation were met only with brief glares and a hostile, stony silence. Leaving this disapproving wall of two, we turned back to the main road, and were soon joined by a well-dressed woman in her early thirties, evidently on her way back home from work. It seems she'd caught the last part of our interaction with the two old ladies and so made a point of overtaking us, and striking up a conversation. As it turned out, she'd grown up nearby, and still lived in the neighbourhood. She explained that, although shikumens were still being torn down all across the city, they had, at the same time, now become quite popular, and many people, both Chinese and foreigners, had started buying up what few remained. Many in the neighbourhood had changed hands in the last year, the last less than a week ago, to an Australian couple, and the two old women, seeing two more foreigners, no doubt assumed we'd come looking to buy another.

It was this younger woman who, hearing about my grandmother's connection to Shanghai, and our resulting interest in shikumens, suggested we go see Xintiandi, a new commercial development recently opened in a large block of restored shikumens not far from the edge of the old French Concession, and a half-hour's walk at most from the hotel where we were staying.

✤

Xintiandi, literally "New Heaven and Earth," is a now well-known upscale shopping and residential complex covering the two-square-block area in the

Luwan district of the old French Concession between South Huangpi Road (formerly Rue Admiral Bayle), Madang Road (formerly Rue Bernier de Montmorand), Taicang Road (formerly Rue Eugene Bard) and Zizhong Road (formerly Rue de Siemen), on the east, west, north and south. Maps of the city from my grandmother's time show a much smaller French Concession, with Rue Eugene Bard as its southern boundary, and the area beyond, including that now occupied by Xintiandi, as open fields.

Built between 1999 and 2001, Xintiandi was part of a wider redevelopment of the surrounding area, one said to have displaced some thirty-five hundred families and led to the demolition of most of the old shikumens in the neighbourhood. The small number of remaining shikumens, which were chosen to house Xintiandi and are in truth quite beautiful, were in fact reconstructed (rather than renovated) from old design drawings, the original bricks and tiles having been preserved before construction and restored to the exteriors upon completion.

The complex is divided into North and South Blocks by Xingye Road (formerly Rue Wantz). On the south side of the North Block, at 76–78 Xingye Road, across the street from the theaters, boutiques, and fitness center, not to mention the luxurious serviced apartments of the South Block's executive residence tower, is the site of the 1921 meeting of the first Congress of the Chinese Communist Party. It was a condition on the granting of the development licence to the Hong Kong firm involved that this site be preserved. The restored site, which is home to the Museum of the First National Congress of the CCP, as a result now shares the North Block with a variety of design-heavy high-end status-saturated venues, and, in much of the Shanghai tourist literature, is presented as just one more item in the glittering array of international brands, chains, designer labels and cuisines laid out there for the visitor's delectation.

The name itself, "Xintiandi," is no doubt meant to call up this profusion of unfolding possibilities. At the same time, it acknowledges certain practical realities, serving to reflect the Party's image of its role in the building of a new, more prosperous China. The grand opening of the North Block was in fact timed to coincide with the lead-up to the eightieth-anniversary celebrations of the founding of the CCP and the subsequent Shanghai APEC Economic Leaders' Meeting, both held in the twelve months prior to our visit to the city. The Xintiandi we found was, therefore, a still-gleaming, almost brand-new edifice. People on the move whisked with great casualness from store to store, designer-label shopping bags proclaiming recent purchases, and in the Starbucks on the ground floor of the North Block, affluent younger couples, evidently out on dates, seeing and being seen, sat idling, their poise almost theatrical in its composure, over green teas, lattes and the like.

The exterior, as promised by the woman we'd been talking to, and who, hearing of our interest in shikumens, had sent us here, is indeed recognizably in the old shikumen style, and, with its stone gates (*shikumen*) and narrow alleyways, succeeds in calling up some semblance of the heyday of the old Shanghai — the gaudy 1920s Wallis Simpson decadence — but like many gestures made in a self-consciously "retro" style, it lacks true continuity, and hence remains, if not exactly unconvincing, safely distanced.

Xintiandi, in part perhaps through this deliberate echoing of that long-lost Shanghai, but more through being called up unexpectedly, in this case several years after our visit, in one of those transmutations that occur — whether by misunderstanding, misinterpretation or embellishment — in stories that are casually passed down to us, retains for me an odd connection to my grandmother.

For the last decade or so of her life, my aunt lived in a then-unusual combination of retirement community and residential care facility, one she'd initially moved into with her husband, Jack. As long as they were able, residents lived separately and independently, in individual units, each with its own small garden, but even so it was possible to arrange for meals to be provided, and these would be taken in the facility's communal dining hall. During her latter years here, my aunt wrote to me sporadically, recounting her mother's time in Shanghai, passing on new information as it occurred to her. In one of these letters, apropos of Aunt Jo (whose family name was Seaman, and whose family history, and wealth, she'd been describing earlier), she mentioned that one of the other residents — an old China hand, who'd lived for many years in Shanghai — had told her there was still a "Seaman Road" there, "probably," she added, "where the Seamans had their house." At the time I tried, without success, to find out where this Seaman Road might once have run. It was only some years later, after her death, that a then just published book, *The Old Shanghai A–Z*, allowed me to resolve this puzzle. The book contains a list of all the streets of old Shanghai, giving the current Chinese names, former colonial names, and, where of interest, a short history of each. Though I found no listing for a Seaman Road (or Street or Avenue), in having looked for it among the S's, I discovered Zizhong Road — a street I'd walked on previously, while checking out the architecture of the South Block of Xintiandi — had been, until the Revolution, known as Rue de Siemen. Rue de Siemen. Siemen Road. "Seaman Road" in conversation.

Josephine Seaman — Aunt Jo to my aunt and mother — was born in London in 1872, and orphaned while still relatively young. This must have been a traumatic experience since her original birth name seems not to have been known to even her closest friends in La Jolla, where she lived for the last several decades of her life. It did not, however, prevent her from acquiring an education and, after graduating, she worked at first as a deaconess in the Mildmay Mission in Blackfriars, then one of the poorest parts of London. Through connections made here, she was offered a job in India, as secretary to a bishop. After three years, she moved on to China — apparently attracted to that part of the world by a brother or other relative — and spent the next fifteen years there. While in Shanghai, she taught at a Eurasian girls' school and became acquainted with the Seamans, a childless American couple with a prosperous export business and extensive holdings in New York and Shanghai. It was during this time that she heard rumours of a stranded American girl living "rough" in the mixed Chinese-foreign part of the city. After further enquiries, she made her way into a warren of buildings, up several flights of stairs, and somehow found the room. Eventually my grandmother answered the persistent knocking at the door. By now it was winter, and the room very cold, so Aunt Jo put a pile of coal on the brazier, only later learning that this was my grandmother's entire month's supply.

It was through Aunt Jo, and later on the Seamans, that my grandmother was taken up by the British and American contingents, found a job, and "saved" from her predicament.

The Seamans had always wanted children but been unable to have them, and wanted to adopt my grandmother and Aunt Jo. My grandmother did not choose to accept this offer, but Aunt Jo, who'd had an unhappy childhood, did. My aunt once said, "It always fascinates me that if things had been different our family would have been *very* wealthy — though of course it wouldn't have done us much good since we'd never have been born!"

My grandmother and Aunt Jo retained close ties throughout their lives. My aunt and mother, who were named for them, and who accompanied their mother on her visits there, were frequent guests of Aunt Jo's at the house on Coast Walk in La Jolla. This was especially true after my grandfather's death, when debts still owed by his construction company (most discovered only after an unscrupulous partner absconded, and which, since then, as a matter of conscience, he'd been paying off) left them in straitened circumstances.

Aunt Jo had a reputation for both generosity and loyalty. The former was seen, in her obituaries, to be the result of her own humble beginnings. One such obituary recounts the story of a complete stranger, a young Englishman arrested for overstaying his visa, whose plight she'd read about in the newspaper, and whose best friend she had then invited (in a thoughtful, if somewhat idiosyncratic, gesture) to accompany him as far as San Francisco, where he'd been ordered to report for deportation, arranging and paying for the trip herself. This same obituary was one of several to mention what used to be said in the 1920s of those in search of support for a good cause in the San Diego area, namely that what they needed to do was send out an "SOS" — by which was meant a "Scripps or Seaman." I myself was surprised to discover, talking to my aunt one day, that part of both my mother's and father's medical school fees (this at a time when my father was still only my mother's fiancé) had been paid for by Aunt Jo.

Aunt Jo outlived my grandmother by twelve years and, in that time, must have felt a gradual severing of the connection to their Shanghai days. In 1947, a year after my grandmother's death, she established the Virginia Judy Scholarship (later renamed the Virginia Judy Esterly Award) in memory of her friend. The scholarship was to be given annually to a student in financial need attending Scripps College from either Asia or Europe, and is still in existence today.

❖

The Seaman house in La Jolla, at 1369 Coast Walk, sits on a slope just back from the public path along the coastal bluff overlooking La Jolla Cove. In my aunt's childhood, visitors were forever coming and going, whether to chat, consult, or else engage in various acts of public planning or philanthropy. The house was filled with the hangings and furniture brought back from China by the Seamans when Aunt Jo's adoptive father retired from his export business and returned to upstate New York, and the house where he'd grown up. He died there not long after their return, and when, following the first war, her mother became an invalid, and needed a warmer climate, they decided to move to California, taking the China mementoes with them. They'd originally intended to settle in Coronado but, on the way, stopped at La Jolla for a bite to eat and were so taken with it they decided to remain there. Old family photos show the house, then known as Seacliff House, standing alone on the hillside amidst tall, blowing grasses. Now, hemmed in by other houses, with its street address obscured, it has become difficult to find, except on the seaward side. From the Coast Walk path, it and its neighbours lie behind thick jade plant and jasmine hedges, ice plant beyond these covering the steep hillside garden of the property next door. The house itself can still be clearly seen, with its open octagonal porch, stone chimneys and long banks of windows looking out onto the sea.

All this we discovered in 2009, when we visited La Jolla, nominally on other business, but also on the trail of my grandmother. After our walk along the bluffs, we stopped in at the La Jolla Historical Society, where we had the good fortune to be taken up by the archivist, who provided us with not only a good deal of his time and local knowledge, but also copies of a number of useful documents, including the various obituaries of Aunt Jo. It was in one of these, an excerpt from a three-hundred-page typewritten history called *Inside La Jolla: 1887–1987*, published in 1986 in preparation for the upcoming centenary celebrations, that we came across a brief aside noting that the then-current owners of Seacliff House were still carrying on the tradition of entertainment and philanthropy begun there by Aunt Jo.

The following day we went looking for the house along the street itself, a task complicated by the proliferation that had taken place over the intervening decades. Newer multi-million-dollar houses, shielded behind various impenetrable plantings, burglar-proof fences, high walls and alarm systems, were packed in cheek-by-jowl down both sides of the street. After much to-ing and fro-ing, we brushed aside the foliage of an overhanging shrub, found the address and, lifting the latch of the small gate, entered the property, where with some trepidation I knocked on the front door, but received no answer.

It's strange to be bequeathed someone else's memories. My mother, as a natural aspect of her personality (and despite a demanding career), appeared always to drift through life, and so it was with no particular purpose, and in no particular order, that she spoke of things that had taken place before I was born. She spoke not to impart information, but as an accompaniment to some ongoing inner experience. Her recollections, as a result, were fewer in number and less detailed than my aunt's, and stand out all the more strongly for having been passed down in casual conversation. I am now quite possibly the sole remaining guardian of a few such memories, memories I had no part in making, each at once both commonplace and singular. Many involve food, and all took place after the girls' father's death, invoking what seemed for my mother a distinctly earlier California, still embedded in the present. Once, out of the blue, in the midst of tipping and tailing beans, she stopped suddenly to comment that whenever they visited La Jolla, they became so overstuffed with "French finery" — the rich sauces and endless courses prepared by Aunt Jo's cook — that they were left famished for ordinary food and, immediately on their departure, would set upon plain bread, hard cheese and crackers, and the like. A second story concerns an excursion they'd taken — where, and for what purpose, she no longer remembered. They'd been driving for some hours in the hinterlands, growing hungrier and hungrier, no towns in sight, hence nowhere to stop to eat, when all at once their mother spotted an isolated farmhouse, set back some distance from the road. Stopping to enquire, she disappeared into an open doorway and returned with a freshly baked apple pie and bowl of clotted cream. Another time, driving in an open-topped car to Arizona, newly outfitted in denim jeans, and nibbling on the wild blackberries they'd stopped to pick along the way, it rained, and when the three of them undressed that night, their legs were bright blue!

Aunt Jo never married, though, according to my aunt, there was a ribbon-tied packet of letters that was to be destroyed, unread, upon her death. This meant she had no children of her own. My grandmother, for her part, had two. The first, my mother, was named Josephine in Aunt Jo's honour, while my aunt was called Virginia, like her mother. It's only now, on recording these notes, that I'm struck by the deliberateness of that second gesture — as if, in this act of naming, some part of that friendship, forged in Shanghai out of such precarious circumstances, might be passed down, by a kind of sympathetic magic, to another generation, and so given an autonomous existence.

My mother passed on to me one more quite vivid picture from that time, of driving down the California coast with my father, on their way to La Jolla. The cars in those days, she explained, had no heaters, so instead they set off with steaming-hot baked potatoes in the pockets of their coats.

⌖

Not long after I last saw my aunt in person, I received a short note with a detail I'd not heard before. The story had been told her by Aunt Jo. After getting her job and being taken up into the Seamans' circle, my grandmother was rapidly swept up into the social whirl that was the life for well-off Westerners in the

Shanghai of that time. She'd become engaged to W. W. Taylor and, at a ball, while dancing with him, "saw" my grandfather (who was still back in Berkeley) entering the room. She broke off her engagement and soon left for home.

My aunt wrote: "Later she asked my father what he had been doing that night. He told her he'd been overwhelmed with the need for her, and gone up to the hillside where they'd often sat together, and longed for her. It was, of course, the spot on which they built their home."

This was the house my aunt and mother both grew up in, and where I did also, in my turn.

❖

There is a postscript to these stories of my aunt's. It was sent in a letter posted shortly before her death, which was at first mis-delivered, then redirected, so it did not reach me until after I'd learned the news of her passing in a phone conversation with my sister, who'd been in frequent contact with her in her last few months. My aunt had been through a difficult time. Her husband Jack had died finally, after a long, debilitating illness, and it was obvious her own approaching mortality was much on her mind. She began the letter by saying how glad she was that the little she knew, but which she treasured, would not die with her, then went on to recount a trip they'd made when she was two or three years old and her sister — my mother — five or six.

They'd gone by train from Berkeley to New York to visit Aunt Jo, who by then had returned from China with her adoptive parents. The journey across the country had taken two weeks, and been a great adventure. The Seamans were living in a grand house in Poughkeepsie, with an attached farm whose primary purpose was to supply food to the big house. She and my mother had been provided with a nanny for their stay there. Despite how young she'd been, my aunt could still remember something of the train trip, and the splendour of the Seaman house, which apparently contained many of the elaborate furnishings the Seamans had acquired in China, and which would later become fixtures of the house on Coast Walk in La Jolla.

Some time after my aunt's marriage, when Jack was teaching for a few years at an eastern college, they'd taken a trip to Poughkeepsie to find the old mansion and farm. This turned out to be easier than they'd anticipated, since people in the area were still well-disposed toward the family, and happy to talk to those, like them, who showed an interest in it. The mansion, they discovered, was now a rest home, while the farm proper had been sold, the land broken up to provide building lots for houses, sometime in the period just after the second world war. The house had been donated to the YWCA while the land was generally held to have gone for a knock-down price. My aunt's impression was that this had been another of Aunt Jo's well-known charitable gestures. After they'd driven past the house, and through the neighbourhood that once had been the farm, they pulled in at a local restaurant for tea, and learned the woman who had been their nanny was still living in the area. Stopping to visit, they'd been astonished to find she still remembered the two girls, and kept a photograph of them, standing in their party dresses on the front verandah of the big house, on her mantelpiece.

One late afternoon, 5 p.m. or so, in summer, as we were crossing Tiananmen Square, we saw an old man standing by himself in this vast public space gazing steadily upwards. For a moment we might have wondered if he were lost, but then we could see that in his hands he was holding a spindle, attached to which, and climbing up into the sky, was a long, nearly invisible strand, at the very end of which was a kite. As far as we on the ground were concerned, it was a windless day, but the kite felt the winds that were blowing on high. How this elderly, in truth rather fragile-looking, man had succeeded in raising this kite, or how long he had been there, we were not to know. It was a box kite, a type common in China, but although common, each one, custom-built and hence shaped by the owner's hand, is itself extraordinarily individual, and takes to the wind in its own way. The shadows had begun to slide across the square; it would soon be dark; but the kite would have a long time yet in the sun. And I thought: a piece of paper with writing on it is flat, but when what is written on that paper fills the mind of a reader, it takes off into the wind and sun like a box kite on a windy day. With some of Lu Xun's surfeit of hope then, we have titled these proto-stories, these essays, or memoirs, or prose poems, *Box Kite*, imagining that the two dimensions of a piece of paper might transform in the mind of a reader into something filling three, or even four, dimensions, assuming time may be counted on as the fourth.

This book was written collaboratively, out of shared experience. That said, experience like narrative is mutable, and the narratives contained herein, we hope, reflect this understanding, being *true* — true, that is, to the best of our knowledge, abilities, and intentions, and in this way tethered to life, which continues after the book ends.

Except where otherwise explicitly noted, the translations from Chinese are by Baziju, and any mistakes therein, in consequence, our own.

We close with a few notes on points not already touched on in the pieces themselves.

"Tengluo: Wisteria" is for Liu Yuxiang.

"The Snow Cabbages of Harbin": The East Garden restaurant is, at last report, still to be found in the Fernwood district of Victoria, B.C. Thanks to Hao Baicai.

"Summer Day in the Mountains": Li Bai (also known as Li Bo, or Li Po) lived in eighth-century Tang Dynasty China, and is widely considered to be, if not the greatest, then indisputably among the greatest, of all Chinese poets.

"Xishi Doufu": Xishi (pronounced roughly *See-sure*), the legendary beauty of the Chinese Warring States Period (475–221 BCE), was the favourite concubine to Fuchai, the last king of the State of Wu, and one among the many prizes gifted to him as tribute by the State of Yue after the defeat of Yue and capture of its king in battle. The eventual destruction of his kingdom by the resurgent State of Yue is widely held to be a consequence of Xishi's bewitching of Fuchai, and the subsequent neglect by him of the affairs of state. A number of Tang Dynasty poets, Li Bai among them, wrote poems in which Xishi appears. These were widely interpreted at the time as veiled commentaries on the then-emperor's favourite concubine, Yang Guifei.

"The Garden of the Master of Nets" is for Andy Patton.

"Harbord Street": Harbord Street, in Toronto, runs from the University of Toronto at its eastern end to Ossington Avenue on its west, a distance of a kilometer or two.

"Liquidambar: Adelaide Hills": The southern-hemisphere hills referred to here are those of the eastern suburbs of the city of Adelaide, in the state of South Australia.

"*Songshu*" is for Luo Hui.

"*Yuanfen*": The Torrens is the main river running through the city of Adelaide.

"My Friend Liu": The "Thousand Buddhas" here refers to the small glazed figures covering the surface of the Duobao Liuli Pagoda, a three-storey tower not far from the top of Longevity Hill in the Summer Palace in Beijing. During the Cultural Revolution, the heads of those within reach of one person sitting on another's shoulders were systematically vandalized, leaving the lowest rows composed entirely of regular arrays of headless yellow figures meditating peacefully against a green tile background. The pagoda was left in this state for more than thirty years, and repaired finally only in 2008, during the lead-up to the Beijing Olympics.

"Yard": The yard in question makes an appearance also in Eirin Moure's (Erin Mouré's) *Sheep's Vigil by a Fervent Person*.

"Lu Xun's Desk": Lu Xun (1881–1936) is one of the great short story writers in any language. He was a major figure in the Baihua movement, which altered forever the course of Chinese literature, and is considered by many to be the greatest twentieth-century Chinese writer.

"The Scholar of the Garden": Cao Xueqin, the author of the novel *Honglou Meng,* was a member of a formerly prosperous bannerman family. He was born in 1715 and died in 1763, and experienced the sudden collapse of his family's fortunes during his teenage years. There have been numerous TV and movie adaptations, and at least eight translations into English, of the novel, under various titles. Among the latter, our personal favourite is that by David Hawkes and John Minford, *The Story of the Stone: A Chinese Novel in Five Volumes* (Penguin Books, 1973–1986, and Indiana University Press, 1979–1987).

"Box Kite" owes a debt of kinship to Ouyang Xiu.

"Shanghai": *Shikumen* (pronounced roughly *sure-koo-mun*) first appeared in Shanghai in the 1860s, their construction being a response to the rapid increase in population associated with the influx of refugees from various nearby provinces fleeing the ravages of the Taiping Rebellion. The form is a hybrid of the southern Yangtze courtyard house and Western row-house styles. A typical shikumen complex consists of a series of two-to-three-storey houses lining both sides of an alleyway, each joined to its neighbour, and each with its own small "courtyard" (in later versions, often just a front yard protected from the street by a high brick wall). The entrances to most shikumen alleyways are surmounted by large, often ornate, stone arches. It is these "stone gates" that are thought to give the shikumens their name. At the height of their popularity, over eighty per cent of the population of Shanghai lived in such complexes.

In an odd closing of the circle begun with Virginia Esterly (née Judy)'s time in China, the youngest of her great-great-grandchildren, daughter of her daughter's daughter's only son, bears the middle name Shanghai, in homage to her mother's family origins.

Finally, thanks to Liu Yuxiang, Luo Hui, and Andy Patton, not only for their friendship, but for the particular quality of that friendship, which lends credence to the unexpected, and hence gives rise to books.

ACKNOWLEDGEMENTS

Thanks to Janice Gurney and Andy Patton for lending their visual acuity and judgement to the editing of the images included here. Additional thanks to Andy Patton for the alchemistry of their translation into black and white.

This book benefited from the close reading of André Alexis, who brought a rigorous prose eye to bear on the prose of this poetry and poetry of this prose.

Thanks to Stuart Ross for his ear, expertise, and forbearance, and to Anansi for a generosity of spirit which has made the publication process a pleasure.

Thanks also to the following for support through the Ontario Arts Council's Writers' Reserve program: *Arc Poetry Magazine*, Black Moss Press, *Brick: A Literary Journal*, Brick Books, Wolsak and Wynn Publishers.

This work was produced with the support of the City of Toronto through the Toronto Arts Council.

Further thanks to the following, in which sometimes earlier variants of the pieces in this book first appeared: *Brick: A Literary Journal*, *Descant*, *Exile*, *Lake: A Journal of Arts and Environment*, *Numero Cinq*, *Prism International*, *The Warwick Review*.

"My Friend Liu" was produced as a limited-edition broadside, designed by Robert MacDonald, and screen-printed by Briar Craig, as part of the celebration for the launch of *Lake*.

The Stephen Owen quote at the front of the book is from *Traditional Chinese Poetry and Poetics: Omen of the World* (University of Wisconsin Press, 1985).

The quote which ends "Xishi Doufu" is from Gu Hua's postscript to the 1987 Panda Books edition of *A Small Town Called Hibiscus*, translated by Gladys Yang.

The quotes from Shen Zongqian and Hayden White in "The Scholar of the Garden" are from *Jie zhou xue hua bian* (Renmin Meishu Chubanshe, Beijing, 1962) and *The Content of the Form: Narrative Discourse and Historical Representation* (The Johns Hopkins University Press, 1987).

The book *The Old Shanghai A–Z* mentioned in "Shanghai" is by Paul French, published in 2010 by Hong Kong University Press.

A few remaining variant usages will be found in this book. These are deliberate and meant to notate specific vocal choices, and are not the result of any lack of diligence on the part of Anansi's expert copy-editors, who remain aware, and no doubt justifiably unsettled, by their continuing presence.

ROO BORSON is the author of ten books of poetry, including *Short Journey Upriver Toward Ōishida*, which won the Governor General's Literary Award for Poetry, the Griffin Poetry Prize, and the Pat Lowther Memorial Award. She has also been involved in a number of collaborative projects, including *Introduction to the Introduction to Wang Wei* by Pain Not Bread (Roo Borson, Kim Maltman, and Andy Patton).

KIM MALTMAN is a poet and theoretical particle physicist. He has published five collections of solo poetry, including *Technologies/Installations*, been involved in three collections of collaborative poetry, and published over 170 papers in the scientific literature. As a member of Baziju, he is also engaged in an ongoing project translating selections from the works of the Tang Dynasty poet Li Bai and Song Dynasty poet Su Shi (Su Dongpo) into English.

BAZIJU (Roo Borson and Kim Maltman) is the composite author of various collaboratively written works of poetry and translation.